BACK TO LIFE

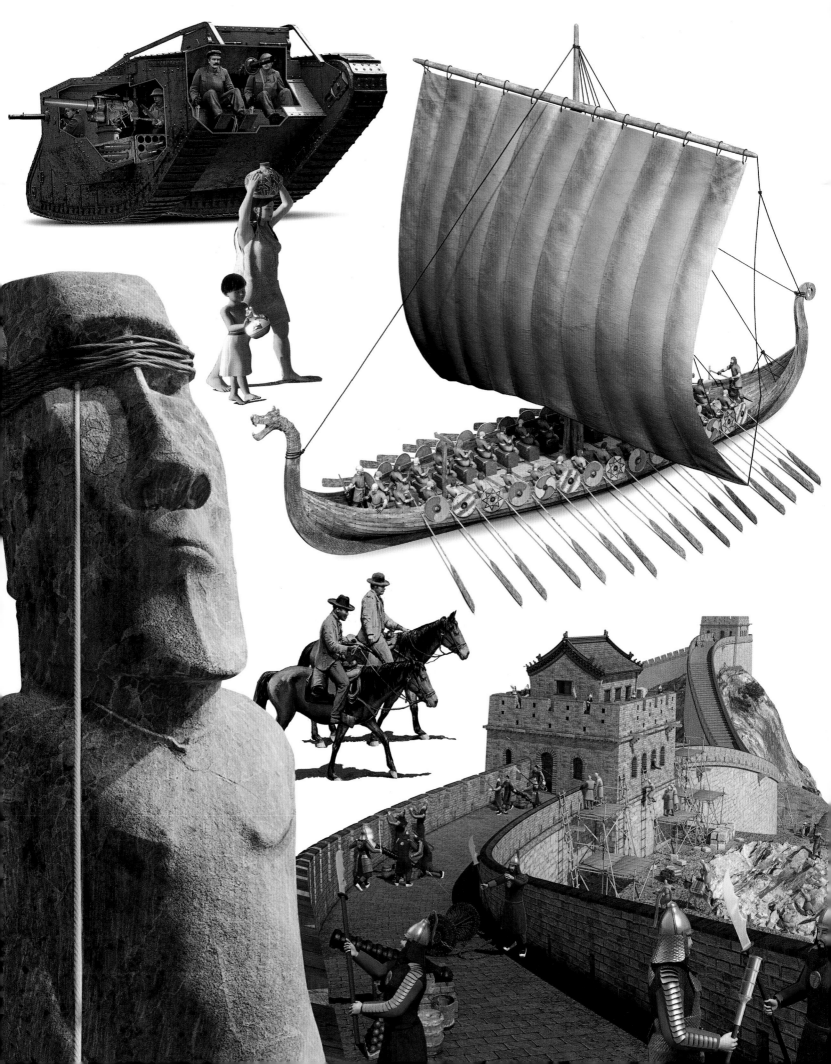

BACK TO LIFE

DK

DK | Penguin Random House

Senior Editors Sam Kennedy, Anna Streiffert Limerick
Senior Art Editor Sheila Collins
Senior US Editor Megan Douglass
Editorial team Michelle Crane, Camilla Hallinan, Georgina Palffy, Justine Willis
Design team Mik Gates, Rachael Grady, Jim Green, Beth Johnston, Kit Lane, Gregory McCarthy
3-D illustrators Art Agency (artists: Barry Croucher, Jean-Michel Girard), ArtistPartners: Angelo Rinaldi, Gary Hanna, KJA Artists, Arran Lewis, Peter Bull Art Studio, SJC Illustration, Sofian Moumene
Picture Researcher Sarah Hopper
Creative Retouching Steve Crozier, Stefan Podhorodecki
Managing Editor Francesca Baines
Managing Art Editor Philip Letsu
Production Editor Jacqueline Street-Elkayam
Production Controller Sian Cheung
Senior Jacket Designer Suhita Dharamjit
Senior DTP Designer Harish Aggarwal
Senior Jackets Coordinator Priyanka Sharma-Saddi
UK Jacket Designer Akiko Kato
Jacket Design Development Manager Sophia MTT
Publisher Andrew Macintyre
Art Director Karen Self
Associate Publishing Director Liz Wheeler
Publishing Director Jonathan Metcalf

Contributors Ian Fitzgerald, Lizzie Munsey, Rona Skene

Specialist Consultants Dr. Maria Fernanda Boza Cuadros; Danièle Cybulskie; Dr. Sona Datta; Dr. Vivian Delgado; Dr. Dydia DeLyser; Professor Peter Doyle; Professor Joann Fletcher; Paul Greenstein; Dr. Piphal Heng; Katharina Hersel; Francisco Torres Hochstetter; Stephen Kay, FSA; William Lindesay, OBE; Professor Lloyd Llewellyn-Jones; Tim Maltin; Dr. David Petts; Michael H. Piatt; Dr. Martin Polkinghorne; Dr. Natasha Reynolds; Professor Michael Scott; Dhananajaya Singh; Christine C. Spiller; Dr. Stephen Turnbull; Professor Stephanie Wynne-Jones; Marie Kesten Zahn

First American Edition, 2022
Published in the United States by DK Publishing
1450 Broadway, Suite 801, New York, NY 10018

A catalog record for this book is available
from the Library of Congress.
ISBN: 978-0-7440-5039-4
Printed and bound in the UAE

For the curious
www.dk.com

MIX
Paper from responsible sources
FSC™ C018179

CONTENTS

TIME TRAVEL

From the ruined Roman city of Pompeii in Italy to the great Cambodian temple complex of Angkor, the world is filled with clues to the secrets of the past. This book explores just a few of these amazing places and what they can tell us about the people who came before us.

4. Wreck of *Titanic*
About 12,500 ft (3,800 m) below the freezing North Atlantic lies the ocean liner *Titanic*, which sank on April 15, 1912.

1. Rapa Nui
This island in the Pacific Ocean, administered by Chile, is famous for the giant statues built on its volcanic slopes.

BODIE
US

WHYDAH SHIPWRECK
US

2. Spruce Tree House
Deep in the canyons in the southwest of the US, the Puebloan villages of Mesa Verde are built into cliffside alcoves.

3. Machu Picchu
The Andes mountains of Peru are home to this Inca city that may once have been a royal palace or religious center.

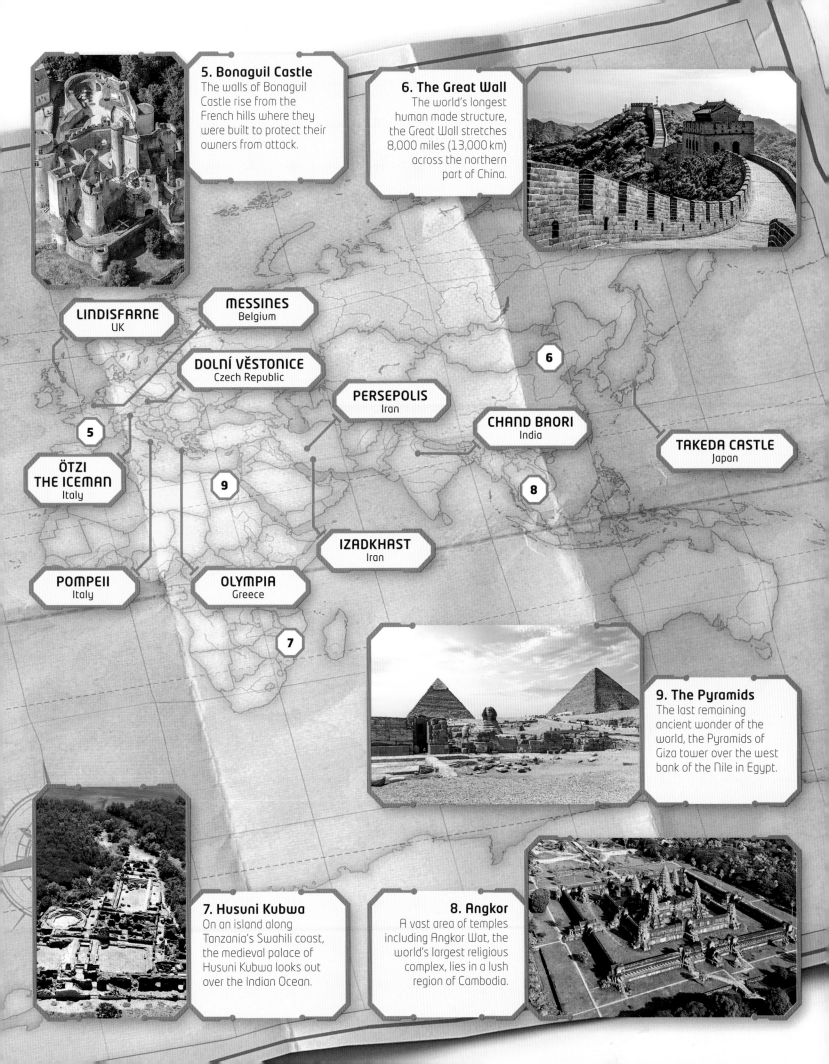

5. Bonaguil Castle
The walls of Bonaguil Castle rise from the French hills where they were built to protect their owners from attack.

6. The Great Wall
The world's longest human made structure, the Great Wall stretches 8,000 miles (13,000 km) across the northern part of China.

LINDISFARNE
UK

MESSINES
Belgium

DOLNÍ VĚSTONICE
Czech Republic

PERSEPOLIS
Iran

CHAND BAORI
India

TAKEDA CASTLE
Japan

5

ÖTZI THE ICEMAN
Italy

9

8

IZADKHAST
Iran

POMPEII
Italy

OLYMPIA
Greece

7

6

9. The Pyramids
The last remaining ancient wonder of the world, the Pyramids of Giza tower over the west bank of the Nile in Egypt.

7. Husuni Kubwa
On an island along Tanzania's Swahili coast, the medieval palace of Husuni Kubwa looks out over the Indian Ocean.

8. Angkor
A vast area of temples including Angkor Wat, the world's largest religious complex, lies in a lush region of Cambodia.

STONE AGE CAMP

Hidden under soil for tens of thousands of years, Dolní Věstonice was once a busy camp, inhabited by about 100 Stone Age hunters. The settlement here was built around 30,000 years ago. Archaeologists excavating it have found human burials, ceramic figures, and the remains of ancient homes.

Stone Age sites
Dolní Věstonice is in the Pavlov Hills near the city of Brno in the South Moravian area of the Czech Republic. It is not the only discovery of its kind, several other Stone Age sites have been found in the vicinity of Dolní Věstonice.

Triple burial
The skeletons of three male teenagers were discovered at Dolní Věstonice. They were buried touching each other, alongside necklaces, red ocher powder, and a mammoth bone.

The skeleton on the right was buried with its left elbow over the body in the middle.

Prehistoric art
Statuettes of female bodies have been found at Stone Age sites across Europe. They were carved from stone or ivory or shaped in clay. This figurine from Dolní Věstonice dates from approximately 28,000 BCE, making it one of the oldest pieces of ceramic art yet to be discovered.

The statuette is made of fired clay. It is 4¼ in (11 cm) tall.

The body on the left was positioned with its arm reaching out.

Carbon dating
All living things contain carbon but, after they die, it begins to break down. Archaeologists use carbon dating to find out the age of old bones and other artifacts by measuring how much carbon is left in them.

Bear sculpture
Clay was readily available near Dolní Věstonice. People used it to make models of animals, such as this bear. Once sculpted, the models were baked in campfires to make them harden and keep their shape.

An archaeologist takes a sample from a human leg bone.

The bear's head is held low, with its neck stretched forward.

Hidden history

So much time has passed since Dolní Věstonice was inhabited that the remains here are deeply buried under layers of earth between the hills and the river. The site was first discovered in 1922, and excavations have continued ever since. A museum has been built to teach visitors about the site and the lifestyles of our Stone Age ancestors.

The Pavlov Hills rise up behind the Dolní Věstonice site.

The river provided the people who lived at the camp with a source of water.

What is farmland today would once have been swampy scrubland.

Reconstructed hut

Stone Age people lived in round, animal skin-covered structures, with wooden poles for support. A fire in the center would have kept the hut warm but inside it would have been smoky.

1 Mammoth
A female mammoth has been separated from the group. She rears up to defend herself.

2 Mammoth herd
The rest of the mammoth herd makes its escape, toward the distant hills.

3 Stay down!
Hunters crouch to stay back from the mammoth while looking for a weak spot to strike.

4 Attack
The hunters prepare to throw their spears at the mammoth to avoid getting too close.

5 Clothes
Simple clothes made from hide offer the men little protection against the mammoth.

6 Dog
The hunters are accompanied by a number of tame dogs who help them hunt.

HUNTING A MAMMOTH

A herd of mammoths is passing through Dolní Věstonice. This is good news! A mammoth can feed a large number of people. However, catching one is difficult—people can easily be killed by a swinging tusk or stamping foot. Today, a group of hunters and their dogs are brave enough to try their luck.

Hunting spear
Hunters are likely to have used small pieces of flint inserted into an ivory or bone handle as a spear. These would have been sharp enough to pierce an animal's tough skin.

Sharpened flint tips the spear.

Mammoth beasts
As this reconstructed mammoth skeleton shows, mammoths were bigger than modern elephants, with much longer tusks. Females and their offspring lived together in herds.

An intricate pattern has been carved into this mammoth bone.

Carved tusk
Mammoth tusks were used for making tools, jewelery, and weapons. This one has been carved with swirling lines that might be a stylized depiction of a human body.

Bone necklaces
This image of a face was carved into a piece of bone. It is one of several sculptures of human faces found at Dolní Věstonice.

The simple lines depict a human face.

Reindeer horns could be used to make tools.

Hunting the herd
As well as mammoths, the people of Dolní Věstonice hunted reindeer as the beasts moved between their summer and winter grazing areas. Some of the meat was preserved for later.

7 Reindeer
Herds of reindeer graze on the hills. They would be good to eat if the mammoth escapes.

8 Settlement
The hunters live in homes grouped together in a small village for protection.

CAVE PAINTINGS

These hands were painted on the walls of the Cueva de las Manos (Cave of the Hands) in Argentina between 13,000 and 9,500 years ago. The people who created them used a hollow bird bone to blow paint over their hands. Some of the hands are small and probably belonged to children.

ÖTZI THE ICEMAN

One fall day in 1991, two Germans hiking in the Alps stumbled across a human head and torso emerging from the melting ice. That body turned out to be 5,300 years old. Along with tools found at the same site, the frozen body was so well preserved that archaeologists have pieced together clues to bring his story to life and solve the mystery surrounding his violent death.

The Iceman's grave
Hikers found the Iceman on the Italian-Austrian border. His last days had taken him from the subalpine region of the Ötztal Alps and up to the Tisenjoch Pass.

Bracken fern

Sloe berries

Einkorn

The last supper
By examining the contents of the Iceman's stomach, scientists discovered he ate ibex (wild goat) for his last meal. His diet also consisted of einkorn (an early type of wheat), venison, and sloe berries. Traces of bracken fern were also found in his stomach, which he may have taken as medicine.

The Copper Age
The first of the metal ages is known as the Copper Age. This was a time when people began to extract and smelt metal to mold into tools rather than using stone. Remains of copper tools and arrow heads have been found in the region where the Iceman died.

Ötzi's autopsy
Archaeologists studying the body revealed it to be of a 45-year-old man with brown hair, who weighed about 134 lb (61 kg). Forensic examinations also suggest that he was in poor health, that he suffered from sore joints, and that he bled to death. Due to the pollen of a hop hornbeam tree found on his body, scientists could also tell that he died in early summer.

Rescuing the body
After the German hikers made their shocking discovery, a rescue team attempted to free the body from the ice. Despite the aid of a pneumatic chisel, the body wouldn't budge. It was not until a few days later that a second rescue team was finally able to dislodge the corpse and it was sent away for a regular autopsy in Austria.

Snow and ice
The body laid buried in snow and ice, which stopped it from decomposing. Even its eyeballs were found to be intact.

Mystery man
At first people thought the corpse belonged to a missing hiker, but at the autopsy scientists made the astonishing discovery that the body was 5,300 years old!

The Ötztal Alps
The Iceman is named Ötzi after the mountain range where he was found. He died at a height of 10,530 ft (3,210 m) in the Central Eastern Alps region known as the Ötztal Alps.

1 Ötzi's attacker
Hiding behind a rock, a mystery assailant aims his bow and arrow at Ötzi and shoots.

2 Backpack
In his rush to flee, Ötzi has left his larch and hazel backpack with hide sack behind.

3 Flint dagger
Inside a sheath tied to his belt, Ötzi carries a flint dagger with an ash-wood handle.

4 Belt and pouch
The leather strip around Ötzi's waist keeps his coat in place, and also holds tools and a pouch.

5 Tattoos
Ötzi's body is covered in 61 tattoos, made by rubbing soot into small cuts in his skin.

6 Arrow
The flint arrowhead hits Ötzi's shoulder, mortally wounding him. In a few minutes he will be dead.

> **"Everything we know** about clothing from the **Neolithic age** in Europe is from him. There is nothing to compare. **He is alone.**"
>
> —Dr. Markus Egg, Archaeologist (b. 1954)

ÖTZI AMBUSHED

It's early summer, over 5,300 years ago. Ötzi, a hunter from a farming community in the Ötztal Alps, is scrambling up a glacier. Despite being well-prepared for the hostile terrain, it's been an exhausting few days. He's being pursued by an attacker who wounded his hand with a knife. He's already escaped once but now, as he flees higher up the mountain, he senses there might be danger around the corner. It turns out he was right.

Birch-bark containers are lightweight but very strong.

Birch-bark containers

Lying close to Ötzi's body, archaeologists found two round containers made of birch bark. The containers were made from a single piece of bark and stitched together with fibers from a lime tree. Inside one of the pots, maple leaves and charcoal flakes were discovered, suggesting Ötzi used the containers to carry charcoal embers wrapped in leaves so he could start a fire quickly and easily.

The container's base was made from a round piece of birch.

Early acupuncture

Ötzi is the world's oldest known tattooed mummy. Tattoos of lines and crosses were located on his body where he would have suffered joint pain. Scientists think they were a form of pain relief.

The blade was bound to the handle with leather thongs.

Status symbol

The copper-headed ax that Ötzi was carrying when he died was a symbol of the high status he held in his community. The ax would be used for felling trees, cutting ice, and as a weapon. It is the only complete prehistoric ax to have been discovered.

Leather straps tied the outer and inner layers of the shoe to the sole.

Comfy shoes

Ötzi's shoes would have been warm and comfortable, although they would not have kept his feet dry from the rain. The outside of the shoes were made from deerskin, with a bearskin sole. Inside, a woven-grass netting held a layer of hay in place for warmth.

7 Clothing
Well-prepared for the freezing conditions, Ötzi wears garments made from goat and sheep skin.

8 Copper Ax
Ötzi's most treasured possession is his ax, made of yew with a copper blade.

THE PYRAMIDS

Dozens of tombs and temples dot the desert sands at Giza, but they are all overshadowed by three colossal stone pyramids. These great structures were built as tombs for pharaohs, who were the rulers of ancient Egypt. The pyramids are an astonishing feat of engineering—they were built more than 4,500 years ago, using little more than muscle power.

Riverside site

Giza is located on the lower stretch of the Nile River, which flows north into the Mediterranean Sea. The site sits at the edge of the modern Egyptian capital, Cairo.

The falcon behind Khafre's head is a symbol of Horus, a god who protected the pharaohs.

River transportation

The ancient Egyptians used the Nile River to transport materials. At the time, water was the only way to carry heavy loads over long distances. Stone was brought along the Nile from elsewhere in Egypt to adorn the tombs and temples at Giza.

Khafre forever

Pharaoh Khafre was one of the rulers of ancient Egypt's Old Kingdom. He reigned from around 2558 to 2532 BCE. Ancient Egyptian rulers sought to live on through the buildings and statues they left behind. Khafre had over 300 statues of himself made for a temple beside the pyramid.

Treasure for the afterlife

Many royal and important people were buried or entombed in smaller tombs near the three large pyramids at Giza. They were buried with precious items, such as gold and jewelery.

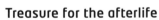

These bracelets were found in the tomb of Khafre's grandmother, Queen Hetepheres I.

The Great Pyramid of Khufu is the tallest of the three pyramids at Giza. The smallest pyramid (not shown) is that of Menkaure, which was also the last to be built here.

Khufu's son Khafre built his pyramid on higher ground than his father's, so it appears to be taller than it is.

The Great Sphinx is 66 ft (20 m) tall, with a human head on the body of a lion.

Revealing the tombs

Archaeologists have been working at Giza for over two hundred years. Today, parts of the site that were once covered by sand have been excavated. It is possible to walk through temple ruins, enter tombs, and follow narrow passageways to the burial chambers inside the pyramids. New artifacts and even tombs are still being found in the area..

Digging at Giza

Excavation work is still ongoing at Giza. Archaeologists today work to find out more about the people who built the pyramids, as well as the pharaohs buried inside.

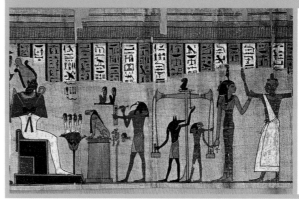

THE AFTERLIFE

Ancient Egyptians believed that life continued after death. Here, the god Anubis weighs the heart of a dead person against a feather to decide if they are evil or good enough to go on to the afterlife.

BUILDING OF GIZA

The sun has barely risen, but work is already underway on Khafre's pyramid. Teams of workmen hurry to put the finishing touches on this enormous tomb. In the meantime, Khafre and his entourage have arrived to inspect the progress. They sit comfortably, away from all the dust and sweat of the building site.

1 Sphinx
The Sphinx's head is being carved out of a piece of rock sticking up from the desert.

2 Khafre's tomb
The pyramid is nearing completion. It should be ready and waiting for Khafre when he dies.

3 Khufukhaf I
The Pharaoh's vizier (prime minister) is also his brother. He looks over the plans.

4 The Queen
Khafre's sister and wife, Khamerernebty, compliments him on his burial complex.

5 Pharaoh
Khafre is pleased with the progress. This pyramid should ensure his immortality.

6 Shady seating
Pharaoh Khafre and his queens enjoy the shade of a shelter put up for the inspection.

7 Ramps
Huge blocks of stone are hauled up ramps to reach the higher levels of the pyramid.

8 Examination
New blocks of stone have just arrived. Stonemasons check them for flaws.

9 Mastaba
This flat-roofed tomb, known as a *mastaba*, is being built for Khafre's brother, Khufukhaf I.

10 Great pyramid
The vast tomb of Khufu, Khafre's father, looms over Giza, dwarfing everything below.

11 Queens' tombs
Royal women, such as Khafre's mother, Queen Henutsen, had smaller pyramids of their own.

12 Rollers
Wooden rollers are placed under the stone blocks, making them easier to pull along.

IN THE GREAT PYRAMID

Khafre's father, the Pharaoh Khufu, knew that the treasures buried with him would be tempting for grave robbers. So, he had his pyramid designed with several layers of defense, hoping that thieves would be unable to get in once his burial chamber was sealed. Unfortunately for Khufu, his defenses were not enough to dissuade the grave robbers—his chamber is thought to have been plundered within a few hundred years of his death.

The capstone at the very top of the pyramid may once have been covered in gold.

Five chambers are stacked on top of the King's Chamber, to relieve the pressure on it from the mass of stone above.

The nine granite slabs that form the ceiling of the King's Chamber are 18 ft (5.5 m) long and weigh around 25-40 tons each.

The King's Chamber
At the heart of the pyramid is Khufu's burial chamber. It is lined entirely with red granite, and holds a matching granite sarcophagus (stone coffin). Three huge blocks of granite were used to close off the entrance to the chamber.

This statuette of Khufu is made of ivory. It was found at Abydos, Egypt.

Construction blocks quarried from the surrounding desert rocks form giant steps beneath the outer layer of white limestone.

Pharaoh Khufu
Khufu was the first pharaoh to build a pyramid at Giza. His is the biggest of them all. It is precisely aligned north–south and almost a perfect square.

This chamber is known as the "Queen's Chamber," but was never meant for a queen—they have their own pyramids.

Funeral boat

In 1954, an Egyptian archaeologist found a dismantled wooden boat buried in a pit near the Great Pyramid. Symbols carved on the pieces made it easier to put it back together. The boat may have been used to carry the pharaoh's body during his funeral.

This model of Khufu's boat shows how it looked when it was pieced together.

Smooth, carefully cut and polished white limestone covers the surface of the pyramid, making it gleam.

The grand gallery

The grand gallery
This is the largest space in the pyramid, with a length of 153 ft (47 m) and a 28-ft- (8.6-m-) high roof. The gallery rises very steeply up toward the King's Chamber.

This passageway was the only way into or out of the tomb. After entombing the pharaoh, priests left the pyramid along it, sealing the exit behind them.

2.3 million blocks of stone were used to build the **Great Pyramid.**

A passage leads to another burial chamber carved into the rock underneath the pyramid. It may have been originally intended as Khufu's burial chamber, or to confuse grave robbers.

Canopic jars
Egyptian bodies were mummified (dried out and wrapped in cloth) for burial. The body's organs were too wet to be mummified, so they had to be removed first. The organs were stored separately from the rest of the body, in containers called canopic jars.

PREPARING A TOMB

To the east of Khufu's Great Pyramid, work is underway on an important new construction—a flat-topped *mastaba* tomb for Khufukhaf I, son of Pharaoh Khufu and brother to Pharaoh Khafre. Khufukhaf is a member of the royal family, so his tomb is being constructed by expert craftsmen.

Brightly colored paint has been applied to these finished carvings, bringing them to life.

Life story
Carvings on the walls of the tomb depict scenes from Khufukhaf's life. Here he is shown receiving offerings for his use in the afterlife. The carvings are plain now, but would originally have been painted in bright colors.

Goods for the afterlife
Tombs were filled with everything the dead person might need in the afterlife. This included clothing, furniture, food, and jewelery. Ordinary people had simple grave goods, while royalty had the finest things available.

Gold chair buried with Queen Hetepheres I

Working by oil lamp
Egyptians used lamps made from bowls filled with oil, with a twist of linen for the wick. Tomb artists generally used plant oils, such as sesame and castor, and added salt to stop the oil from smoking and spoiling the paintings.

Hieroglyphs

The ancient Egyptians wrote using a series of stylized pictures, called hieroglyphs. In tombs, they were used to write stories about a person's life and family. Inscriptions in Khufukhaf's tomb explain that he was the vizier (prime minister) of Egypt and the son of a queen.

Painting materials

Ancient Egyptian paintbrushes were bundles of grasses or reeds tied together with string. Most paint was made from natural rock pigments—for example, iron oxide produced yellows, ochers, and reds. One color, Egyptian blue, was synthetic. It was made by mixing and heating minerals at a high temperature. This made it very expensive.

Skilled artists sketch out images onto the freshly plastered walls of the tomb.

A stonemason carves into the wall, following drawings made by the artists.

Tomb painting

Painting tomb walls with images such as this boat on the Nile was often a lengthy process. Craftsmen plastered the walls and artists drew the outlines, adding color at the end.

Mastaba come from the **Arabic** word for **"bench"** because these **tombs** were **bench-shaped**.

HAULING STONE

Huge blocks of stone for Pharaoh Khafre's new pyramid have arrived from the harbor. Teams of men place them on sleds for hauling to the pyramid. The heaviest stones aren't just dragged—a series of wooden rollers are placed under them. New rollers are added in front of the sled as the team pulls it along.

Plumb bob
The pyramids were built accurately using simple tools made of wood, string, and stone. This is a plumb bob. It was hung from a string on a wooden A-frame to make a level. When the string aligned with the center of the A-frame's crosspiece, the surface it sat on was level.

This man is trying to direct the hauling teams so they don't crash into each other.

Stonemasons' tools
Limestone was smoothed using copper chisels. The stonemason held a chisel in one hand and pounded it with a wooden mallet. Workmen had to stop and resharpen their tools often, so there were full-time tool sharpeners on hand to support them.

MALLET

BASKET

Stone masons shape the blocks, making sure they are smooth.

Wooden sleds are used to move the huge stone blocks.

CHISEL

"The mouth of a **perfectly contented man** is filled with **beer**."
—Egyptian proverb, c. 2200 BCE

This amulet shows the Eye of Horus. It is carved from a mineral called carnelian.

Protective amulet

Amulets were believed to have protective powers, which would be passed on to the person who wore them. Shapes and colors had specific meanings—for example, the Eye of Horus symbolized healing, and orange-red carnelian was for energy and power.

Water is poured in front of the sleds, making it easier for them to run.

Fine jewelery

Ancient Egyptian men, women, and children wore jewelery. They were also buried with it, in the hope of taking it to the afterlife. This carving shows metalworkers making a wide, beaded necklace that would have sat across the wearer's collar bones and chest.

It takes two workers to carry these heavy jars. They must be careful to avoid spillages.

Brewing beer

Beer was a common drink in Ancient Egypt, often drunk by laborers. Many brewers were women, like the one in the tomb model below. They made beer by crumbling bread into water and leaving it to ferment in jars. Dates and honey were added to sweeten the drink.

Each block of stone weighs around 1.8 tonnes.

EGYPTIAN TOMB PAINTINGS

The tombs of wealthy Egyptians were covered in complex, colorful paintings. The images told stories about who was buried in the tomb and what they needed to do to pass through the afterlife. In this painting on a tomb in Thebes, the dog-headed god Anubis is preparing a body.

PERSIAN PALACE

Nestled in the remote mountains of Iran is Persepolis, a grand ruined city that was once the ceremonial capital of the Persian Empire. This complex of palaces and temples may not have been occupied all year, but at the New Year, subjects visited from around the empire to pay tribute to the emperor.

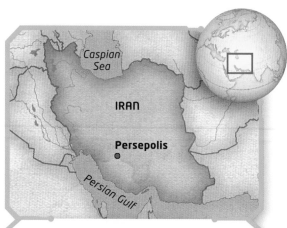

Heart of an empire
Persepolis was established near the center of the Persian Empire, in what is now Iran. The empire expanded from this area into eastern Europe and northwest India.

Darius I
Persepolis was founded by the Emperor Darius I in 518 BCE. He divided the Persian Empire into provinces called satrapies. Once a year each satrapy had to show their loyalty by sending valuable gifts to the emperor.

This ornate gold and silver metalwork is in the shape of a winged goat.

The swirling pattern represents the figure's curly hair.

This sculpture was made from lapis lazuli, a semiprecious stone prized for its intense blue color.

A royal head
This tiny figure is believed to show the head of a Persian queen or perhaps a young prince. It is one of the few artifacts to survive Alexander the Great's attack on Persepolis.

Treasured tribute
This figure of a leaping goat would once have been one of two handles on an elaborate vase. It was part of a gift offered to the emperor as tribute. Each of the Persian satrapies had to send tribute. If they failed to do so, they would be severely punished.

The Apadana

The main audience hall in Persepolis was called the Apadana. Tribute bearers would climb the grand staircase, then be received by the emperor and offer him their gifts. Along with much of Persepolis, the Apadana was destroyed by Alexander the Great in 330 BCE. It then lay forgotten for almost 2,000 years before it was rediscovered in the 17th century.

Once, 72 65-ft- (20-m-) tall columns supported the roof of the Apadana.

Carved images of Persian warriors decorate the walls of the palace.

Foundations

Two golden tablets were found buried under the foundations of the Apadana. The writing on them outlines the territories of the Persian Empire and thanks the Persian god Ahura Mazda in three different languages.

AHURA MAZDA

The Persians followed the Zoroastrian religion. They believed in a god called Ahura Mazda—"wise lord." This carving from Persepolis shows Ahura Mazda as a man rising up from a winged disk.

CELEBRATION

A festival atmosphere bubbles through Persepolis—it is Nowruz, the New Year celebration, and hundreds of people have brought tribute to the emperor. The city is crowded and noisy, it bustles with people and animals from across the empire. Persian officials oversee the excitement as the visitors wait to enter the Apadana.

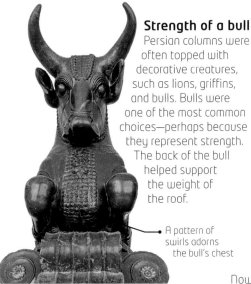

Strength of a bull

Persian columns were often topped with decorative creatures, such as lions, griffins, and bulls. Bulls were one of the most common choices—perhaps because they represent strength. The back of the bull helped support the weight of the roof.

A pattern of swirls adorns the bull's chest

This horn is decorated with the snarling head of a lion.

Drinking horn

Nowruz was a lively event and a time for celebration. Some of Persepolis's visitors might have used the time to enjoy a drink from a *rhyton*, an elaborate drinking horn.

Living gifts

Carvings at Persepolis show that people brought animals from all over the Persian Empire as tribute. This frieze shows Bactrians from Central Asia with a camel to present to the emperor.

Chariots and roads

The Persians used chariots on an extensive network of roads they built to help them control their enormous territory and move soldiers and goods quickly and easily from one place to another. This tiny golden figurine of a chariot shows a local governor visiting a province under his control.

This figure is thought to be a *satrap*—a local governor.

Four horses pull the chariot

1 The Immortals
The emperor is guarded by a troop of highly-trained elite soldiers, called the Immortals.

2 Bactrian camel
This camel has walked all the way from Bactria in Central Asia to be given to the emperor.

3 Gifts from the south
These men from Nubia, south of Egypt, have brought ivory and an exotic animal: an okapi.

4 Wait your turn
People climb the steps in order—those from near the center of the empire go first.

5 Distractions
These courtiers have been distracted on their way into the Apadana by the action below.

6 Drink break
This Scythian from the north is enjoying a drink in the middle of the celebrations.

7 Managing the crowd
Two Persian officials try to keep the procession moving. Their chariot is a good vantage point.

8 Precious dust
A man from Sindh (modern-day Pakistan) carries jars full of valuable gold dust.

9 What's that smell?
With all these animals around, there is dung everywhere. You might want to hold your nose!

10 Angry mother
This big cat has been brought as tribute. She is furious her cubs have been taken away.

11 A dangerous game
A Scythian plays with a lion cub, not realizing its angry mother is just in front of him.

IMMORTAL WARRIORS
The most elite Persian soldiers were the Immortals. They led attacks on the battlefield and formed the emperor's personal bodyguard. This mosaic from the Persian royal city of Susa shows a heavily-armed group of Immortals equipped with spears, bows, and quivers full of arrows.

THE OLYMPIC GAMES

In the rolling hills of the Greek countryside, beside a sacred grove of olive trees, lies Olympia, a sports ground dedicated to the god Zeus. Every four years from 776 BCE to 393 CE the Festival of Zeus was held here, accompanied by the Olympic Games, the cultural high point of the Greek calendar.

1 The stadium was where athletic events such as races and javelin throwing took place.

GREECE

Aegean Sea

Ionian Sea

Olympia

Birthplace of the Olympics

Olympia is in the Peloponnese region, in the south of mainland Greece. The site is located where two rivers meet, a short distance inland from the Ionian Sea.

The athlete has his arm back, ready to swing it forward and release the discus.

2 The Hill of Kronos was covered with oak trees and olive trees, both sacred to Zeus.

Sporting ideals

Ancient Greece was made up of city-states that constantly fought each other. Most sports were based on the skills needed in war, such as speed and strength. The Greeks also prized beauty, discipline, and honor, and the Olympic Games celebrated all of these ideals. Athletes were often portrayed in sculptures, such as this discus thrower.

This sculpture shows the strong, athletic physique valued by the ancient Greeks.

The glory of Zeus

The Greeks believed in gods and goddesses with a wide range of powers. The Olympic Games were held to honor Zeus, King of the Gods. He was also God of the Sky and Keeper of Oaths, responsible for order and justice.

3 The Temple of Hera, Queen of the Gods, was the first temple built at Olympia, in the 6th century BCE.

4 The Temple of Zeus was the most important Olympic shrine. Built in the 5th century BCE, it housed a huge statue of Zeus.

5 The palaestra was where boxers and wrestlers trained. It was built in the 3rd century BCE.

Written evidence
Much of what we know about the ancient Olympics comes from the detailed written accounts of early travelers. One of these was Pausanias, a Greek traveler and geographer who wrote a ten-volume book called *Description of Greece*.

Olympic coins
Special coins were produced for the festival by the city-state of Elis, which organized the games. The coins showed Zeus on one side and his sacred eagle on the other.

THE GAMES

The Festival of Zeus is in full swing. Athletes have flocked to Olympia from across the Greek city-states, eager to show off their sporting prowess. There is plenty for non-athletes to do, too—they listen to orators, watch races, buy food, and catch up on the latest news.

1 Temple of Hera
Dedicated to Hera, wife of Zeus, this temple is the oldest one at Olympia.

2 Offering
An athlete makes an offering to ensure no one cheats in his race.

3 Altar of Zeus
This altar is made from the ash of sacrificial animals. Today, 100 oxen will be sacrificed.

4 Treasuries
These buildings contain valuable objects given as offerings, such as armor and statues.

5 Barbecue
People have lit cooking fires and the smell of roasting meat has begun to fill the air.

6 Stadium
Foot and field events take place here. There is space for 40,000 spectators on the banks.

7 Lines
People are lining up to get a taste of the barbecued meat being prepared at the stalls.

8 Boxing match
The losing fighter raises a finger to admit defeat. Boxers fight naked, with no protective clothing.

9 Statues
Finely carved statues around the site commemorate past Olympic champions.

10 Temple of Zeus
This is the biggest building in Olympia. A colossal statue of Zeus sits inside.

11 Speaker
By addressing the crowd, this orator hopes to make a name for himself.

12 Sacred tree
This man is cutting branches from an olive tree to make wreaths for the winners.

THE STADIUM

The armored race is underway. The banks of the stadium are crammed with spectators who shout in excitement and cheer on the runners. Athletes crash into each other as they circle the turning post on their way to their second length. From the judges' stand, the *Hellanodikai* watch carefully, looking out for any athletes who are tempted to cheat.

Olympic events

Athletics was a key part of the Olympic Games. Events included javelin, long jump, discus, and running races. There were many different races. As shown on this vase, the foot race was run by athletes who were completely naked, not wearing or carrying anything that could slow them down.

This vase shows three runners in close competition..

Race in armor

Athletes ran the armored race wearing heavy helmets, like the one shown here, and carrying shields. The race was a sprint up and down the length of the stadium's field, with a 180° turn around a post after the first length. Both speed and strength were required to succeed.

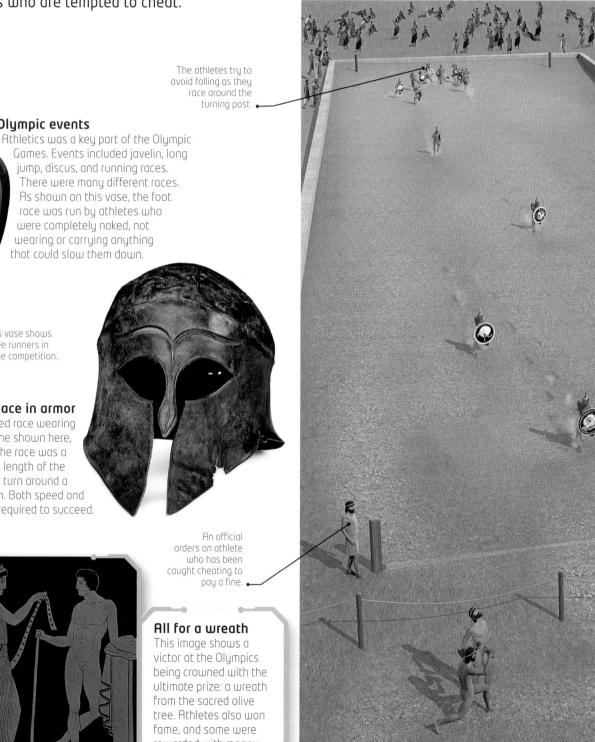

The athletes try to avoid falling as they race around the turning post.

An official orders an athlete who has been caught cheating to pay a fine.

All for a wreath

This image shows a victor at the Olympics being crowned with the ultimate prize: a wreath from the sacred olive tree. Athletes also won fame, and some were rewarded with money.

Spectators jostle each other as they try to get a better view of the track.

The judges sit in this area, where they have a good view of the whole stadium.

The *Hellanodikai*

The organizers and judges of the Olympic Games were called the *Hellanodikai*. They decided who should be allowed to compete, grouped athletes into age categories, supervised training, decided on winners in close races, and punished cheaters.

The *Heraea*

A separate festival was held for women, in honor of the goddess Hera, wife of Zeus and queen of the gods. Only unmarried women could compete and there were three age categories. Winners received olive wreaths.

The athlete lifts her skirt so she can bend her leg.

Jumping aids

Competitors in the long jump carried two stones called *halteres*, one in each hand. As the jumper leapt into the air, they swung their stones forward, to increase their momentum and help them jump greater distances.

Athletes used this hole to help them grip the stone.

TEMPLE OF ZEUS

Finished in 463 BCE, this shrine to the king of the gods is an awe-inspiring building. Its white plaster gleams like marble and its colors are bright and freshly-painted. Inside, an enormous statue of Zeus presides over the temple. It has only been in place for four years, but it is already famous for its size and splendor. A stream of visitors make their way up the temple steps to see the statue and pay homage to almighty Zeus.

The temple is beautifully decorated with bright, eye-catching colors.

Fragments of friezes showing the exploits of the hero Hercules have been found at Olympia.

Six marble columns support the front of the temple.

Herodotus stands below the temple steps, reading extracts from his latest work to anyone who will listen.

People are eager to visit the temple and see the famous statue of Zeus.

Herodotus

The writer and historian Herodotus went to the Olympics in 426 BCE. He stood on the east steps of the Temple of Zeus and read aloud from his *Histories*. Being heard at Olympia could make a writer famous.

"And immediately everyone knew him much **better** than the **Olympic victors** themselves. There was no one who had not heard of the name of **Herodotus**."

—Lucian of Samosata, writing in the 2nd century CE

Pelops and Hippodamia

The carvings on the east side of the temple show the story of Pelops and Hippodamia. Pelops won Hippodamia's hand in marriage after winning a chariot race. He is said to have founded the Olympic Games after his victory. In this image, Pelops has Hippodamia in his chariot.

Zeus holds a statue of Nike, goddess of victory, in his right hand.

In his left hand Zeus holds a scepter topped with an eagle.

Nike of Paionios

Nike was the goddess of victory. This statue of her was reconstructed from fragments found by archaeologists in 1875. Nike is shown as a winged woman in flight, with her clothing blowing around her. The statue was nearly 6½ ft (2 m) tall. It was made from marble and might once have been painted.

Only parts of Nike's arms have been found.

The great statue of Zeus is 42 ft (13 m) high.

The shapes used to create the folds in Zeus' garments can be seen in the mold.

Wonder of the world

In the 20th century, fragments of the clay molds used to make the Statue of Zeus were excavated from the famous sculptor Phidias's workshop at Olympia. This statue became known as one of the seven wonders of the world. After the ancient Olympic Games ended, the statue was acquired by the Romans; it ended up in the city of Constantinople, where it was later destroyed by fire.

ROMAN TOWN

In the early afternoon of August 24, 79 CE, a dark cloud of smoke, ash, and red-hot rock filled the sky above the busy Roman port of Pompeii as the volcano, Mount Vesuvius, erupted. Its ash covered the city, preserving it perfectly. The remains offer a unique insight into how the ancient Romans lived.

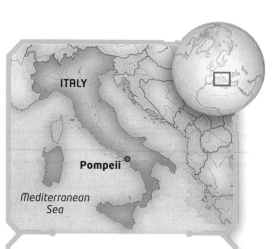

The Roman Empire

Pompeii lay south of Rome, the center of the Roman Empire, in the Bay of Naples. Many of the estimated 20,000 people who lived in Pompeii were full citizens of the empire.

Blue jug

Ash from the eruption of Vesuvius preserved many delicate items, such as this glass jug, in very good condition. By examining the jug, historians can tell how it was made and used.

This blue color was created by adding a mineral, cobalt oxide, to the glass.

This person huddled in a crouched position as the ash fell.

Final moments

The rain of ash that fell on Pompeii quickly set in place around people's bodies where they fell, suffocated by the ash. Over time, the ash and debris hardened. Archaeologists have poured plaster into the cavities left by the bodies to make casts of the dead.

Tools of the trade

To excavate a site, archaeologists must work very carefully. Brushes and picks help them expose their discoveries.

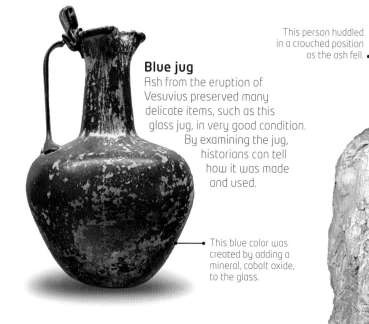

Early exploration

It was always known that there was a hidden Roman city near Naples, but it wasn't until 1748 that excavations began. This photo shows archaeologists at Pompeii in the late 19th century.

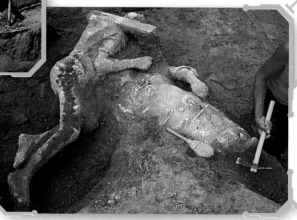

Rooftop remains

The person being excavated here might have been one of the last to die in the disaster. Their body was found on the roof of a villa. They probably climbed up to try and escape the danger.

In the shadow of a volcano

The ancient city walls of Pompeii run for about 2 miles (3 km) around the archaeological site. A modern town, Pompei, has sprung up nearby. Mount Vesuvius, the volcano whose eruption destroyed the Roman city, looms above the ruins. It has erupted many times since the destruction of Pompeii and no one knows when it might do so again.

1 City limits
Pompeii had a perimeter wall to control access to the city.

2 Grid plan
Many Roman cities were planned on grids, with the roads crossing each other at right angles.

The eruption of Vesuvius

A young scholar called Pliny the Younger watched the eruption of Vesuvius. His eyewitness account inspired later artists, such as Pierre-Jacques Volaire, who painted this dramatic image.

THE LAST DAY

It is August 24, 79 CE. Along the Vicolo dei Vettii, the citizens of Pompeii are talking, shopping, and doing their daily tasks. A black plume of ash rises from the mountain behind them. People are not quite sure what to make of it—should they be concerned? Pompeii has been shaken by earthquakes before but this feels very different.

1 **Rising ash**
The vast ash cloud shooting into the sky is the first warning of the deadly eruption to come.

2 **Shop sign**
Pompeii's shop signs were marked using carvings, such as this one representing a donkey.

3 **Negotiation**
Aulus Vettius Conviva is agreeing a price for repairing a fresco that was damaged in an earthquake.

4 **Settlers from all over**
This North African man is one of many people from outside Italy who make Pompeii their home.

5 **Road crossing**
Roman streets had raised stones, so people could cross the street without getting their feet wet.

6 **Roof repairs**
These tiles were broken in a recent earthquake. There is lots of work for repairmen in Pompeii.

7 **Roman graffiti**
Modern people weren't the first to graffiti. This writing begins "Secundus greets his Prima."

8 **Bakery**
Pompeii is home to at least 35 bakeries—it's easier to buy bread than to bake it at home.

9 **Snack bar**
Most people don't have their own kitchens. They buy food at snack bars, like this one.

10 **Crash!**
This enslaved person has dropped a pot of olive oil, a common ingredient in Roman cooking.

11 **Dry pump**
No water is coming from the pump. Earthquakes might have damaged the aqueduct.

PANIC IN THE BAKERY

The baker is used to the heat. He's been at work since the early hours and is carrying on as normal. Around him, though, people are worried. Why is the earth shaking? And what is that plume of ash doing above the mountain? Perhaps it is time to flee the city just in case there is any danger.

Ancient bread
This loaf was found in a baker's oven in Herculaneum, a town near Pompeii. The heat of the eruption turned it to carbon, preserving it. The stamp on the left is the guarantee of the bread's quality.

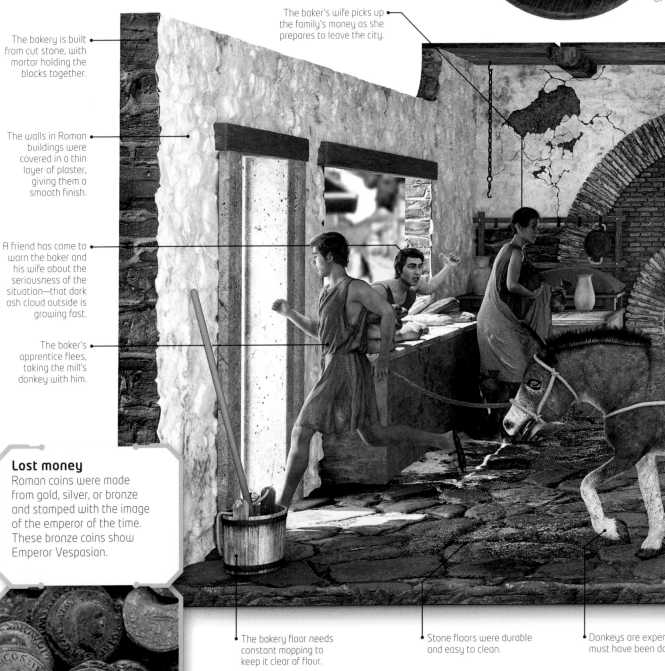

The baker's wife picks up the family's money as she prepares to leave the city.

The bakery is built from cut stone, with mortar holding the blocks together.

The walls in Roman buildings were covered in a thin layer of plaster, giving them a smooth finish.

A friend has come to warn the baker and his wife about the seriousness of the situation—that dark ash cloud outside is growing fast.

The baker's apprentice flees, taking the mill's donkey with him.

Lost money
Roman coins were made from gold, silver, or bronze and stamped with the image of the emperor of the time. These bronze coins show Emperor Vespasian.

The bakery floor needs constant mopping to keep it clear of flour.

Stone floors were durable and easy to clean.

Donkeys are expensive—the baker must have been doing well for himself.

These coins are from a hoard of 1,385 that were found hidden in a large clay jar.

"People **bewailed their own fate** or that of their relatives, and there were some who **prayed for death** in their **terror of dying**."
—Pliny the Younger, Roman author (62–113 CE)

From grain to bread

Roman bakeries milled their own flour, which they then used to bake bread in huge wood-burning ovens. A large bakery usually housed several mills. Each mill had two giant stones, which ground grain between them. The stones would be turned by a donkey, horse, or human.

This mill would be turned by a donkey, but the animal has been set free.

Keeping a baker's oven hot required a lot of wood.

This man is waiting to see what happens before he decides whether or not to leave.

Even the finest Roman flour was coarse compared to what we use today.

THE GOD OF FIRE

The ancient Romans had many gods, including Vulcan, the god of fire. The Romans worshipped him in the hope he would stop volcanoes erupting. They held a festival of Vulcan every year on August 23, called the Vulcanalia.

The dog was wearing a studded bronze collar.

Final moments

Romans kept dogs as pets as well as for guarding their property. This dog was tied up when Vesuvius erupted. Unable to take his collar off or escape, he died at his post.

THE TAVERN TREMORS

This tavern is a popular place for Pompeiians to buy a meal or a jug of wine. Normally, people would be catching up on the latest news while they order, but today the atmosphere is uneasy. The usual earthquakes are happening more frequently, and people are beginning to get scared.

Many Roman businesses painted their names on their buildings.

The remains of carbonized figs

Walnuts

Takeout toppings
Pompeiians ate lots of fruit and vegetables, along with fish, nuts, olives, and lentils. The eruption turned some food to charcoal, perfectly preserving it for thousands of years.

Over the counter
A Roman snack bar was called a *thermopolium*. It sold fast food, ladling out ready-cooked meals from big terra-cotta pots that were set into the countertop. Popular meals included soups, stews, and bread and cheese.

Everyday jug
Most people would have used plates, cups, and jugs made of clay, or bronze if they were wealthy. This jug in the shape of a chicken might have held water or wine.

Busy repairing the roof, this man has only just noticed the size of the ash cloud above town.

Sieve

Ladle

Urn

Cooking tools

The cook in a *thermopolium* had to feed large numbers of hungry people. They used a range of tools to help them do this swiftly and effectively, including tongs, juicers, and ladles. Many of the tools would have been made from bronze.

Wall paintings

The Romans decorated their walls with paintings called frescoes. The walls were plastered, then painted quickly while the plaster was still wet. The colors were fixed in place as the plaster dried.

The water pump is decorated with a carving in the shape of a bull's head.

Garum was stored and transported in tall terra-cotta jars called amphorae.

Fish sauce

Garum was the Romans' favorite sauce. It was made from fish, fish guts, and salt mixed together and then left to rot. Making *garum* must have been a very smelly process.

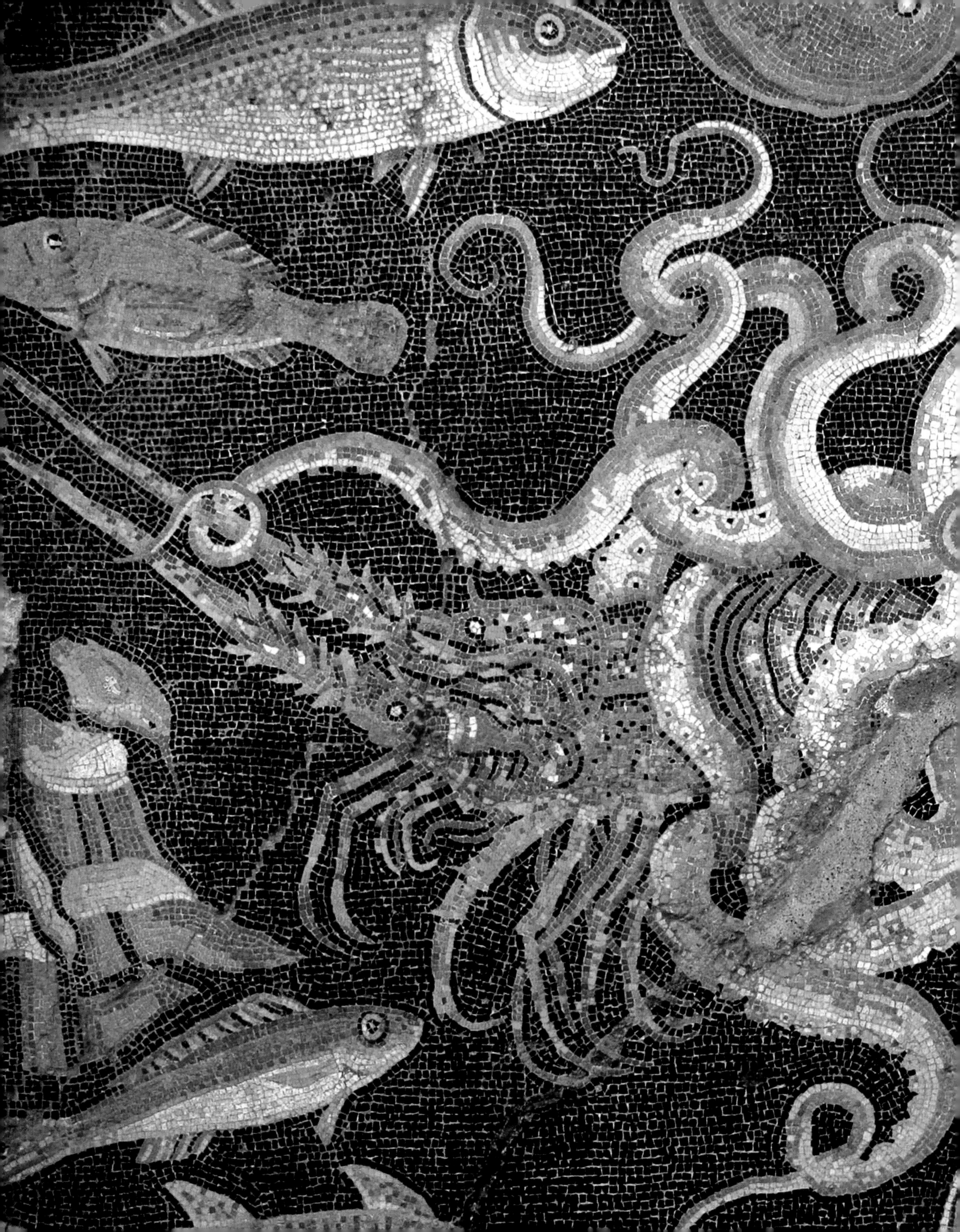

MARINE MOSAICS

The grandest Roman buildings had walls and floors decorated with mosaics—patterns made from tiny cubes of glass, stone, or pottery. This richly detailed example, which features some of the Romans' favorite seafood, was discovered at the House of the Faun in Pompeii.

MEDIEVAL MONASTERY

Once a flourishing monastery (a community of Christian monks), Lindisfarne was the scene of one of the first Viking raids in Britain. Almost nothing is visible of the original buildings today so archaeologists are digging deep into the landscape to find clues about this once-famous center of Christian learning and art.

North Sea

Lindisfarne

UK

A king's gift

Lindisfarne island lies close to what is now England. The monastery was founded in 635 CE by King Oswald, ruler of the Anglo-Saxon kingdom of Northumbria. He asked a monk called Aidan to set up a community there. The new monastery was located only a few days by sea from Scandinavia—the home of the Vikings.

Ring of copper

Ring of bone

Rings and remains

This pair of rings was found around a fragment of finger bone—probably belonging to a pilgrim (religious traveler) who died at the monastery.

Anglo-Saxon cash

These coins, from Northumbria and the nearby kingdom of Yorkshire, were of high value. Lindisfarne was rich and attracted many wealthy visitors.

This coin shows the head of an Anglo-Saxon king.

Carved stone

Name stones were used at Lindisfarne to mark a burial place. This one was made from sandstone at around the time of the Viking raid. It would have been brightly painted and may have had a jewel embedded in it.

The stone is carved with "Osgyth," a woman's name.

The ruins of the 12th-century priory overlook the site of the earlier Anglo-Saxon monastery.

Island excavations

The Viking raid in 793 did not end the Christian community at Lindisfarne. Monks continued to live there and, about 500 years later, a new priory was built on the site, the ruins of which can still be seen today. Archaeologists now run regular digs to uncover the layers of the island's history.

Game of stones

This tiny piece of blue and white glass is a playing piece from a strategic board game a bit like chess called *tafl* (pronounced "taffle"). It may have been buried along with a wealthy local man or woman. The Vikings played a version of *tafl*, too—the game was popular all over northern Europe.

The "crown" of five white dots means this was probably a king piece.

Viking ironware

Unlike materials such as cloth, iron tools and weapons can survive centuries underground. This Viking sword would once have had a leather binding around the handle to make it easier to grip, but that has rotted away, leaving the iron behind.

The cross guard protected the warrior's hand in battle.

1 Rampant raider
This Viking is chasing after a monk who has run away with one of the church's treasures.

2 Dormitories
The monks' and pilgrims' living quarters have been ransacked and set ablaze.

3 Church
The church is made of stone, so it won't burn like the other buildings, which are wooden.

4 Villagers flee
People from the village that has grown up around the monastery flee from the raiders.

5 Captives
Prisoners are lined up to be taken to the ships. They face a hard life of slavery in Scandinavia.

6 Horse horror
Outside the blacksmith's shop, a horse that was waiting to be shod rears up in terror.

THE VIKING RAID

As the summer sun sets on Lindisfarne, a fleet of strange ships slips stealthily into the harbor. Within a few hours, this peaceful place will be reduced to a pile of smoking ruins by rampaging invaders hunting for loot and captives.

7 Self-defense
The blacksmith uses his heavy hammer to try to keep the raiders away from the forge.

8 Shock tactics
A raider wields his sword against a villager trying to defend his home and family.

9 Stone cross
The carved cross honors St. Cuthbert, bishop of Lindisfarne, who is buried here.

10 Holy scripture
A monk begs his captors not to steal the holy manuscript he has worked on for months.

11 Pig on the loose!
A piglet has escaped from the farm. Medieval pigs were smaller and hairier than pigs today.

12 Setting sail
This Viking longship has raised its sail and is ready to head home to Scandinavia.

ST. CUTHBERT

Some 100 years before the Viking raid in 793, King Oswald of Northumbria in northern England made a monk called Cuthbert Bishop of Lindisfarne. After Cuthbert died, many miracles were reported by people who prayed at his tomb in Lindisfarne. Within a few years, the island monastery was attracting thousands of Christian pilgrims.

Center of devotion
The grandest of several churches in the monastery complex, the main church was the busy heart of the community. Monks attended prayers here throughout the day, and a steady stream of visitors came to pay their respects at the shrine of St. Cuthbert.

Anglo-Saxon churches are beautifully decorated inside, with painted walls and arches.

This Viking is about to catch a fleeing monk.

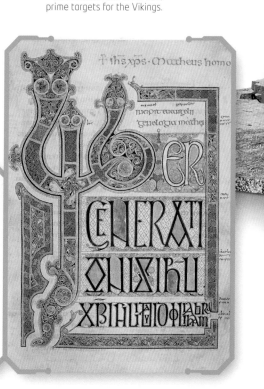

The altar is covered with golden candlesticks and crucifixes, prime targets for the Vikings.

Treasure chest
Churches kept their most precious objects in highly ornate chests. This example from Italy is made of silver and decorated with religious figures.

Novice monks snatch up precious scrolls to try and protect them from the Vikings.

LIFE ON LINDISFARNE

The island of Lindisfarne is tiny, but the monastery is famous in the Christian world. Thousands visit to pray and admire the monks' work— beautiful scriptures and richly decorated religious objects. Surrounding the monastery is a busy, prosperous village that is, however, undefended. To the Vikings, the island is the perfect target.

Lindisfarne Gospels
This spectacular book decorated with exquisite calligraphy is believed to be the work of a monk called Eadfrith. It still survives today, only the cover (said to have been covered with gold and jewels) is missing. It may have been stolen in the Viking raid.

Helping horses

Other than traveling by sea, the fastest way to get around Anglo-Saxon England was on horseback. Blacksmiths had an important role to play, making the horseshoes that protect horses' feet and the stirrups that made riding easier.

These rivets fixed the shoe to the horse's foot.

HORSESHOE

STIRRUPS

The rider's foot slots in here, resting on the bar.

Legendary smith

Blacksmiths were highly respected, and were even the heroes of myths and folktales. This casket shows the legend of Wayland (seen on the far left), a blacksmith of great skill who wreaked gory revenge on the king who captured him.

The village forge

The blacksmith was an important member of the village community. At his forge he made and repaired metal objects. Many villagers relied on him to maintain the tools they used each day.

The blacksmith's treasured tools are hanging here for all to see. They will end up in the hands of a Viking.

The roof is made of flammable thatch and the smith must be careful so that no sparks from the furnace set it alight.

Horses are expensive. This one belongs to a local landowner.

The blacksmith's brave assistant is prepared to stand by his master as a Viking races toward him.

The blacksmith spends all day working with heavy metal—he is one of the strongest men in the village. Now he'll use his strength to fight back against the raiders.

This Viking is hunting for swords or anything else that could be used as a weapon.

Everyday items

Iron objects including farming tools, cooking pots, pins, and knives have been discovered at Lindisfarne. Archaeologists have also found weapons such as swords and spearheads.

PIN

THE VIKING LONGSHIP

The Vikings who stormed Lindisfarne sailed hundreds of miles west over the North Sea from their home in Scandinavia. As well as being great warriors, they are brilliant sailors and master shipbuilders. These skills mean they can travel great distances over rough seas.

Battleaxe
The ax was a fearsome weapon, with its sharp, curved blade and long handle, perfect for two-handed blows.

Edge made of hardened steel

Helmet
Helmets were made from iron, often with a visor and nose guard to protect the eyes and face. The inside was padded with cloth, and leather straps underneath kept the helmet in place.

Leather overshirt is stuffed with linen.

Protective dragons
Dragons were powerful symbols to the Vikings. This metal pin shows the head of the dragon Nidhogg who, in Viking mythology, is nibbling away at the roots of Yggdrasil, the Tree of Life, where gods, humans, and giants all live.

The dragon figurehead is intended to ward off evil spirits and scare enemies.

The sail is only used when it is windy. In calm weather, it is rolled up and the rowers must use oars to propel the ship.

Tunic made of chain mail

The ship's narrow hull (body) means it can sail up shallow rivers to raid inland cities.

The deep keel running under the hull keeps the ship stable in rough seas.

Part-time warriors
The Vikings who attacked Lindisfarne were not full-time soldiers—many who joined the raiding party were farmers or fishermen. They wore metal armor if they could afford it—if not, they wore tunics of padded leather.

"The pagans from the **northern regions** came with a naval force like **stinging hornets** and spread on all sides like fearful wolves."

—Simeon of Durham, medieval historian (1060-1129)

VIKING MYTHOLOGY

Vikings believed that gods and goddesses ruled nature and decided their fate. This carved stone shows Odin, the mightiest Norse god, riding his eight-legged horse. He resides in Valhalla, where fallen warriors are rewarded after death.

A sailor operates the steering oar to change the ship's course.

The ship's stern (back) and bow (front) are identical, which means it can reverse without turning around when rowed.

Shields were wooden with an iron center, which protected the hands from blows.

Circular shields
Viking shields were often painted in bright colors to show their owner's connection to a particular clan or leader. At sea, the shields were mounted along the side of the ship to protect the rowers and frighten enemies.

Long, slim oars power the ship through the water.

conttituta e. qua fabule poctari intaltra
mi   nerua que primu ea excogitasse
            muium fuerat hominib: pui
            habet autem stellas
            mo mali in subcan

A tdms adlla   uda serpens plabitur argo.
C onuertans   cumlumine puppim

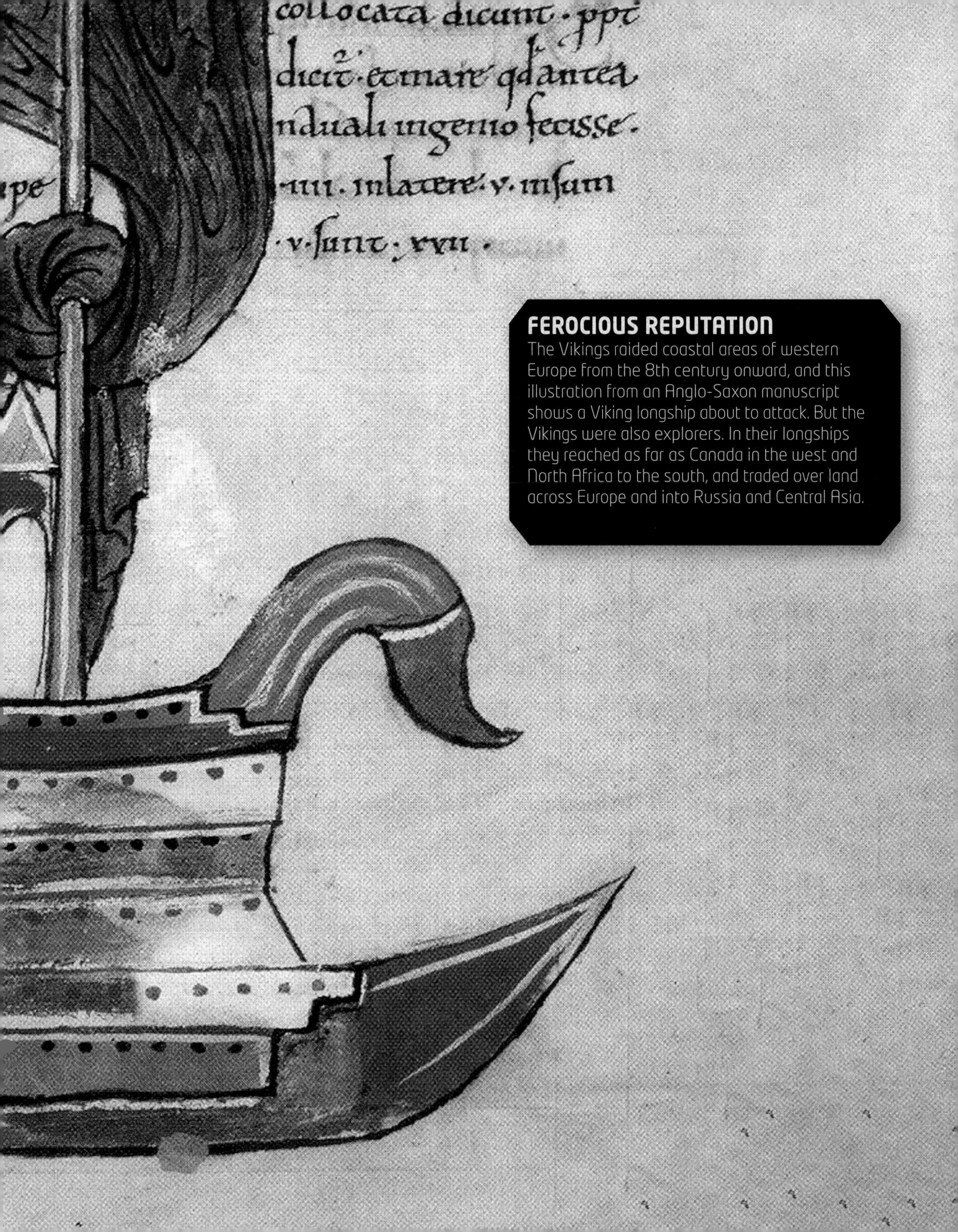

collocata dicunt · ppt
dicit· etmare qd antea
ndiuali ingenio fecisse ·
iiii · inlatere · v · insum
· v · sunt · xvii ·

FEROCIOUS REPUTATION

The Vikings raided coastal areas of western Europe from the 8th century onward, and this illustration from an Anglo-Saxon manuscript shows a Viking longship about to attack. But the Vikings were also explorers. In their longships they reached as far as Canada in the west and North Africa to the south, and traded over land across Europe and into Russia and Central Asia.

INDIAN STEPWELL

Stacks of symmetrical staircases plunge down toward cool water at the stepwell of Chand Baori. It was built in the 9th century by Raja Chanda, ruler of a small Rajput kingdom. Many such stepwells were built across India over more than a thousand years, often by queens for village women. They are beautiful feats of engineering as well as places to collect water.

Northwestern India
The stepwell was built in the village of Abhaneri, in the region of Rajasthan. It is between the cities of Jaipur and Agra, and south of India's capital, New Delhi.

Wells through time
The most ornate stepwells were built in the dry areas of northwest India. As this photo shows, the carved well at Adalaj in Gujarat was still in use in the late 19th century. Once women had filled clay or brass pots at the well, they balanced stacks of them on their heads to climb the steps.

This carving from Chand Baori is of Durga, the Hindu warrior goddess and mother of the universe.

Water gods
Some stepwells are decorated with intricate carvings of gods, goddesses, and water spirits. As well as water sources, stepwells were places where people could pray, meditate, and leave offerings to the Hindu deities. Many stepwells are still used as places of worship today.

Today, a covered walkway with arches runs around the top of the well.

Stepwell design
India's stepwells were designed to help people reach water that lay hidden underground. Often built by wealthy women so village women could gather water, the stepwell's steep walls shaded the deep water, keeping the women cool.

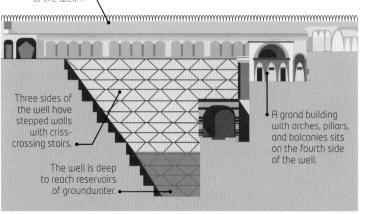

Three sides of the well have stepped walls with criss-crossing stairs.

A grand building with arches, pillars, and balconies sits on the fourth side of the well.

The well is deep to reach reservoirs of groundwater.

Chand Baori today

This ancient well is 100 ft (30 m) deep. It has 13 levels, with 35,000 steps zig-zagging between them. The decorative arches around the walkway at the well's edge were added in the 18th century, when India was ruled by the Mughal Dynasty. Modern railings have been added at the top of the well and midway down, to help keep visitors safe.

1 The buildings around the top were added by the Mughals, who also added ornate pavilions to the well's fourth side. The square well is an inverted pyramid.

2 The thousands of stone steps provided access to the water supply at the very bottom of the well.

Restoring stepwells

Many stepwells had fallen into disrepair. In recent years, groups of women have played a key part in restoring them. They organize repairs and cleaning, making the water safe to use.

GATHERING WATER

It is blisteringly hot at Chand Baori today, so several women from the nearby village are fetching cool, clean water from the well. It is heavy work carrying pots of water up the steps, but the air is cool and the chance to share news with friends makes up for the steep climb.

Palace of Winds
Avoiding the heat has always been important in India. While village women enjoyed the shade of the stepwell, wealthy women appreciated the cool air behind the latticed windows of palaces, such as this one in Jaipur, which was built in 1799.

A balancing act
Collecting water was such a big part of women's lives that it inspired a style of music called Panihari. Still popular today, it is sung by women while dancing with pots on their heads.

It is always women who collect water, not men.

The narrow steps lead down to the fresh, clear water of the well.

The water level rises and falls as groundwater levels vary over the seasons and years.

7

9

Music at the well
On market days and festivals, large groups of people met at the stepwell. Traveling troupes of musicians playing pipes, drums, and string instruments may have entertained them.

1 **Sacred cow**
Cows are holy in Hinduism. This one is resting in the shade of a tree watered by the well.

2 **Singing and dancing**
To lighten their load, women sing of rainfall and romance, dancing to the music.

3 **Musicians**
Music drifts over the well from a practicing troupe, making everyone walk more lightly.

4 **At the well**
Women are arriving at the well. They balance empty water pots on their heads.

5 **Jewelery**
Colorful bangles jingle along the women's arms as they walk.

6 **Social space**
Women chat and catch up on each other's news, enjoying the cool air at the well.

7 **The steps**
Climbing the stairs is hard work, especially with full pots of water on the way back up.

8 **Colorful saris**
The women wear lengths of thin cotton, dyed and printed with bright, beautiful patterns.

9 **Splash!**
Children can't resist the lovely cool water. They jump in and enjoy swimming together.

10 **Ritual washing**
People wash themselves, making sure they are clean before visiting a nearby temple.

11 **Gathering water**
Women dip their pots into the well, letting the cool water flow in and fill them.

SWAHILI PALACE

In around 1300, the Sultan of Kilwa built a palace to prove his power as the leader of one of the most important trading centers on the Swahili coast of eastern Africa. These were part of a huge network that stretched across the Indian Ocean. Ships would sail in on the yearly monsoon winds to trade and only leave when the winds changed. They brought influences from abroad which blended with the rich local culture.

The Swahili coast
Along the coast of east Africa, the Swahili region stretched from what is now Somalia in the north to Sofala in modern Mozambique in the south.

Husuni Kubwa palace was built on the north coast of Kilwa Kisiwani island.

Ruins of Kilwa's Great Mosque, one of the first mosques built on Africa's east coast.

Kilwa Kisiwani island
Islands along the coastline offered shelter from the open sea and became important trading centers. Kilwa Kisiwani had a thriving town and a large mosque, not far from the sultan's palace.

The inscription on these coins is in Arabic.

The text is in rhyme. Rhyming couplets start on one side and finish on the other.

Beads found at Husuni Kubwa, made from glass, clay, and minerals.

Pretty and useful
Beads were used for trade, as well as to make long necklaces for Swahili women. Many imported beads have been found in Kilwa, as well as local beads made from aragonite, a pearl-like mineral from the shell of the giant clam.

Kilwa coins
Coins are useful for trade, so it is not surprising that many were minted in Kilwa. The coins were made from copper and feature poems about the sultan who reigned when they were made.

Archaeologists use a large sieve to look for artifacts hidden in the sand.

Digging up details
Many clues about how people lived in Kilwa are hidden in the ground. Archaeologists sift through the sand and soil, hunting for pieces of pottery, beads, and coins.

Glorious ruins

The spectacular Husuni Kubwa, or "Great Palace," was only used for a short time; it is not known why the sultan abandoned it. The site is now in ruins, but archaeological investigations here have revealed huge amounts of information about Swahili trade and lifestyle. The finds tell of a melting pot of African, Asian, and Arabian cultures.

1 Mangroves now spread out around the site. Once, these would have been managed, leaving a wide waterway leading to the palace.

2 Harvested from offshore reefs, coral stone was used for roofs and wall friezes. It is scattered on the ground where roofs have collapsed.

Pool view

This grand open-air pool was the sultan's private bathtub. Here he had an incredible view out to sea. This was practical, too, as he could watch ships arriving while he washed.

3 The sultan and his family lived in a series of private rooms clustered around a number of interior courtyards. No visitors came to this part of the palace.

4 In this large, open courtyard, goods were collected and traded. Banter and bartering in many different languages echoed around the high walls.

1 The Sultan
Dressed in a long white robe called a *kanzu*, the sultan prepares to take a bath.

2 Hair care
Women from the sultan's family sit by the pool, braiding each other's hair.

3 Merchants
Foreign merchants and dignitaries wait for a chance to meet the sultan.

4 Ibn Battuta
This famous Moroccan traveler is impressed. He writes about his visit in his travel log.

5 Passing time
These merchants play a game of *bao* to keep them entertained while they wait.

6 Busy waters
Dhows of all sizes ply the turquoise waters. Some will stop here, others sail past.

TRADE AND LEISURE

It is 1331, and the sultan's palace is buzzing with activity. Merchants sail in and out, bringing goods from far-off lands. Together with other visitors, they wait in a courtyard in hope of an audience with the sultan. He, however, is in no rush. The sultan is relaxing in his family quarters, preparing to bathe in the cooling waters of his private octagon-shaped pool.

Women's quarters

The women and children of the sultan's family spent their time in the private quarters, away from visitors. Their rooms were very beautiful, with elaborate patterns and niches decorating the walls.

Niches in the walls were filled with precious objects.

This Chinese Yuan Dynasty vase was found in the Husuni Kubwa ruins.

Imported porcelain

Many ceramics have been found at Husuni Kubwa. Fine porcelain was imported from Arabia, Persia, India, and China. Fragments of pottery were often plastered into the palace walls in intricate patterns.

Triangular lateen sail

Pieces made from polished seeds

7 New arrivals
Porters and sailors carry up precious wares from the dhow docked below the steps.

8 Elephant tusks
Enormous tusks from the kingdom of Great Zimbabwe are on show in the courtyard.

Dhow traffic

Cargo boats called dhows criss-crossed the Indian Ocean. They had one or two masts and slanted triangular sails. Large dhows sailed the open ocean, while smaller ones made shorter trips along the Swahili coast.

Bao board

The game known as *bao* in Swahili was popular here in medieval times, and is still played today. Two players take turns to move their pieces around the dips in the board, trying to capture each other's pieces.

MEDIEVAL CASTLE

The walls of Bonaguil Castle tower like smooth cliffs over the French countryside. Every stone of this fortress was placed with the aim of keeping the people inside safe and their enemies out. Many walled castles were built across Europe during the wars of the medieval period. Most were homes and places of work as well as military structures.

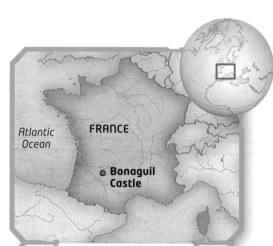

Conflicted territory
Bonaguil Castle is in southwest France, an area that was often fought over in medieval times. Perched on a rocky hill, it has a clear view of the surrounding land.

Siege warfare
Castles were built with thick walls and strong defenses. If the enemy couldn't break through the walls, they would have to surround the castle, then wait for those inside to run out of food, water, and arrows.

A caricature of Viollet-le-Duc, with one of his projects, the Notre Dame cathedral in Paris.

Restoration craze
Many castles fell into ruin during the French Revolution, when many nobles were killed or fled the country.
But in the late 19th century, people began to take an interest in medieval buildings, led by the architect Eugène Viollet-le-Duc. He made drawings of Bonaguil but it wasn't restored as fancifully as some of the castles he visited.

Tiny windows were designed for defenders to shoot arrows from.

Winch

Metal chains

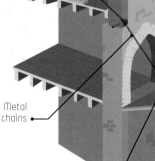

The wooden bridge could be raised by turning the winch to reel in the chains.

Drawbridge
A castle drawbridge could be lifted up, shutting attackers out. It was built across a deep ditch or water-filled moat. Once it was raised, the door to the castle was out of reach.

Stone bridge

Hidden passage
A secret passageway was carved through the rock beneath Bonaguil Castle. It connects a number of defense posts within the castle walls, so defenders could move position undetected.

Changing shape

The oldest parts of Bonaguil Castle are its foundations, which were laid in the 13th century. In the 15th century, the castle was expanded. Improvements included a fortified gateway, drawbridges, and six towers. But by the time the works were complete, France was entering a slightly more peaceful period, and the castle was no longer under threat.

1 This part of the castle was where everyday chores were carried out, such as washing clothes in the laundry and baking bread in the bakery.

Deep well

In the inner courtyard, a well was drilled 157 ft (48 m) down through the rock. It provided all the water the castle needed, so the inhabitants would never run out, even during a siege lasting months.

2 The herb garden was full of plants grown to be used in medicine and to flavor food.

A FESTIVE DAY

The lord and lady of Bonaguil are relieved—the latest improvements to the castle's defensive walls have finally been completed. They have chosen this beautiful day in September 1470 to celebrate, by inviting the local nobility to a joust and a feast. There's a busy fair, too, selling regional specialties.

1 Village
The craftsmen and peasants that work for the castle live just outside its walls.

2 Fair trade
Leather goods, trinkets, tasty apples, hams, and the famous local wine are all selling fast.

3 Here for glory
Knights from other castles prepare their jousting armor with help from their squires.

4 Premium seats
The hosts and their visitors sit comfortably out of the sun, right in front of the action.

5 Just a joust
The noise of clanging armor and heavy hooves is deafening as two knights meet.

6 Barbican
The fortified gateway area in front of the drawbridge is busy with late arrivals.

7 Bridge watch
The guards feel relaxed, chatting about the fine horses while keeping an eye on the drawbridge.

8 Castle core
The keep is the safest spot in the castle. Here people would seek shelter in times of war.

9 Keep it secret
These nobles have found a quiet spot to discuss whether to join a plot against the king.

10 Watch out!
A servant is emptying a full bucket through the window into the dry moat below.

11 Play fight
Two boys are practicing their sword skills. They can't wait to start their knight training sessions.

12 Secret love
A young man is courting one of the castle's ladies by playing the lute and singing of her beauty.

THRILLING CONTEST

To entertain his guests, the lord of the castle has invited famous knights to take on the local champion at a joust. The knights and their horses are dressed to impress. They charge at each other at top speed while the crowd cheers excitedly. Disappointingly, the castle's own knight is not doing well, and is about to take a tumble.

The ridged "comb" along the top of the helmet strengthened it and helped deflect lance blows against the head.

The eye slit allowed the knight to see what was coming toward him.

The visor over the face has breathing holes. It could be lifted up and out of the way.

Protective gear
Jousting knights wore metal plate armor, with chain mail underneath. Jousting armor was more elaborate than armor worn on the battlefield, and it was often intricately decorated.

These fit around the horse's ears, leaving just the tips sticking out.

The eye holes were a weak point in the armor, but the horse had to see where it was going.

This plate protected the horse's forehead and face. It is called a chamfron.

Horse safety
Armor wasn't just for humans. Padded cloth protected a horse's body, with metal plates often worn on the face and neck. It was thought unsporting to deliberately wound an opponent's horse.

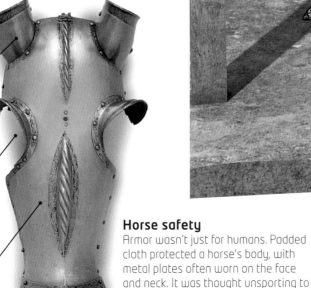

This lady is a chaperone, here to keep an eye on the young lady beside her. She was too busy watching the action and now it's too late to stop the romance.

A young lady offers her sleeve to a knight as a token of her affection.

This knight will wear the lady's sleeve on his armor and joust in her honor.

The horses wear padded fabric outfits called caparisons.

Knights were men tied by oath to fight in wars for their lord or king. When not on the battlefield, they could take part in jousting tournaments.

The wooden lances used in this kind of tournament had blunted tips and were not meant to cause deadly harm.

The local nobles are devastated—their favorite knight has just taken a hit.

Peasants from the nearby village are allowed to watch the joust, but they are not welcome in the comfortable stand where the nobles sit.

This child is desperate to see the fighting up close—his favorite game is jousting knights.

Playing at war

Medieval children were encouraged to play. They enjoyed many types of toys and games, including dolls, balls, stilts, swings, spinning tops, chess, dice, and little action figures such as this jousting knight.

COURTLY LOVE

Noble men and women enjoyed poetry about "courtly love." This was a romantic idea of courtship; the poems told of knights winning over their ladies with beautiful ballads or brave deeds. In reality, the marriages of nobles were arranged by their families.

A barrier fence called a tilt stops the two horses from charging straight into each other.

Each knight had his own family coat of arms. People would know who was who by looking at the coat of arms on the shield.

This horse wears the coat of arms and the red and gold colors of Bonaguil Castle—the knight riding him is the local favorite.

A GREAT FEAST

The joust is over, and the lord and lady of the castle sit down to enjoy a sumptuous feast with their guests. The Great Hall is noisy and full. People shout to be heard over the music, dogs wait for scraps, and wine flows freely. The lord and lady have planned to impress tonight—their best tableware is on display, along with the finest food.

1 Stone castles were always a bit cold, but a roaring fire kept the guests cozy.

2 Tall, pointy hats, inspired by slender Gothic church spires, were the height of fashion at this time.

Salt cellar
Grand tables always had a salt cellar. Salt was highly treasured, and the dish holding it was the fanciest item on the table. Some were shaped like a ship, such as this golden three-master.

3 Dining partners share a plate or a trencher—a thick slice of bread that is used as a plate to hold food. It was considered very bad manners to eat the trencher.

Medieval music
Musicians were hired to entertain guests. During the medieval period, music began to be written down in the way that is familiar to us today, and musicians experimented with new instruments. The most popular stringed instrument was the lute, which is similar to the modern guitar.

4 Musicians are livening up the meal and, later, there will be dancing, too.

5 The most important guests sit with the lord and lady at the raised top table.

Fabulous food

Food presentation was key on feast days. A pig's head served with apples was considered a delicacy. Exotic birds such as swans and peacocks would be cooked and then dressed in their own feathers. Pies and soups were decorated and colored with spices such as yellow saffron, which was very expensive.

6 Less important guests sit at lower side tables. They eat brown bread and drink from pewter cups, while the top table has white bread and cups made of precious metal or glass.

Tapestry

Thick woven tapestries were hung on the castle walls. They kept rooms a little warmer and less drafty. With bright colors and intricate designs, they were also beautiful to look at and often told a story. The famous tapestry shown below, which hangs in a museum in Paris, depicts a story of a lady and a unicorn.

7 A jester capers around between the tables, trying to make the guests laugh.

PUEBLOAN CLIFF VILLAGE

Thousands of years ago, ancestors of the Indigenous people known as Puebloans began to settle in Mesa Verde in the southwest of the US. They were soon building villages, often in deep cliff alcoves which offered protection from the harsh climate. Now partly ruined, these still reveal how Puebloans once lived.

Corn comes in many colors. It can be made into flour when dried.

Mesa Verde

The dramatic landscape of Mesa Verde spreads across the Colorado Plateau, in the state of Colorado, in the southwest of the US. It's near Four Corners, where four states meet: Colorado, Arizona, Utah, and New Mexico.

UNITED STATES

Spruce Tree House

Pacific Ocean

An eagle plume is tied into the dancer's hair.

Favorite foods

Puebloan people began settling and farming in the region sometime around 750 CE. They grew corn, squash, and beans in fields close to the villages. Meat from deer, rabbit, and (later) turkeys, was also on the menu, together with wild berries.

120-room accommodation

Spruce Tree House is one of the largest villages in the area. It has 120 rooms, many of which have two floors as well as a storage level just under the cliff ceiling. There are also eight kivas (underground rooms built for gatherings).

Plan of Spruce Tree House

The natural rock forms the back wall of the village.

Pueblo culture

The Puebloans left the Mesa Verde region in the 13th century, but Pueblo people, and their culture, are alive in Colorado, Arizona, and New Mexico. This young girl, dressed in traditional clothes and ornaments, is performing a ceremonial Kachina dance.

Buildings on the alcove's outer edge overlook the ravine below.

Round plaza with kiva underneath

Sacred object, decorated with an eagle plume

Stolen remains

From the 19th century, a stream of people, from local cowboys to foreign explorers, became aware of the cliff villages. They treated the Puebloan dwellings disrespectfully, looting graves and shipping both human remains and artifacts off to museums in the US and abroad for money.

Remains from a vandalized grave, displayed together with pots and other artifacts.

1 The flat plateau above the cliff, known as the mesa top, is where the Puebloan farmers once grew their food.

2 Sandstone makes up the sheer cliff face. Depending on the light, its color changes from pale yellow to pink-orange.

3 The village was cleverly constructed in a natural alcove in the cliff. Like everything in Puebloan life, it was created in balance with the environment.

4 A deep ravine separates the cliff that holds Spruce Tree House from the taller cliff opposite.

Spruce and juniper trees grow around the village. Juniper was, and is, used in Puebloan ceremonies.

Sandstone bluffs rise up from deep ravines in a landscape shaped millions of years ago.

A home in the rock
Spruce Tree House is one of hundreds of cliff alcove villages in the area known as Mesa Verde. "Mesa" is the name for the sandstone bluffs that dominate this wild region. Many of these feature the natural alcoves that the Puebloans made into homes. In the late 13th century, however, the people who lived here made the decision to move away, maybe due to a severe drought that made life difficult.

Whose land?
Mesa Verde was made a national park in 1906. This was done to preserve the cultural heritage and nature of the area, but the Puebloans—the people who have the strongest connection to the land and know its history—were not consulted in the process. Today, Puebloan people are working toward having the right to manage sacred sites such as Mesa Verde.

PREPARING FOR WINTER

There's a nip in the air this October day in 1270. The village elders have read the signs—winter will come early and be long and cold. Everyone is busy, some with harvesting the last of the corn and squash from the fields on the mesa top, others with preparing supplies and making warm clothes from animal skins. Fires will be lit inside, and drinks of tea made from herbs are served.

Underground kiva

Beneath each round plaza is a circular underground room known as a kiva. It was used for ceremonies and gatherings. It had a fire pit and wall benches, and could hold many people.

Ladder leading into the kiva from the plaza above

Pueblo pottery

The Puebloan people had made beautiful pots, bowls, and ladles for centuries. At this time, they also started producing mugs in the traditional black and white style. All mugs had their own unique geometric patterns.

Clay mug for drinking tea made of herbs

Rock art

The Puebloans carved sacred images in the soft sandstone rocks around their villages. These images illustrate stories of their origins and show animals, human figures, and sacred symbols.

A figure holding its arms up, maybe in a dance.

A *mano* stone is rolled over the corn, crushing it.

Food grinder

Corn and berries were ground to flour or paste on a flat stone called a *metate*. Villages often had a row of *metates* where several women worked side by side to produce food for all.

1 Corn flour
Kneeling on the ground, this woman is busy grinding dried corn kernels into flour.

2 Good harvest
This child is watching her mother prepare the corn. Soon she'll know how to do it herself.

3 Into the kiva
A village elder is stepping down the ladder to prepare a kiva for a meeting.

4 Tasty turkeys
Turkeys run around. They are being fed corn kernels so their meat will taste good.

5 Arts and crafts
This skilled potter is decorating newly made pots with black paint in a fine pattern.

6 Water supply
The girls are coming back from fetching cool, fresh water from a nearby spring.

7 Steady grip
A farmer is climbing up to the fields above the village, using hands and feet to grip the rock.

8 Skillful hunter
A teenage boy proudly returns with rabbits that will provide meat and clothes for winter.

KHMER CAPITAL

Today partly hidden by lush forests, the ancient city of Angkor was once a mighty capital of the Khmer Empire. It was a vast network of temple compounds, palaces, villages, and waterways. Over time, any wooden buildings vanished, leaving behind only gigantic stone temples.

1 The bridge across the moat becomes a raised walkway, which leads through the complex and into the temple itself.

Fertile region
Angkor is in northern Cambodia, in Asia. It is surrounded by forests and farmland. Many rivers flow through this area, watering its many rice plantations.

Gold objects, such as this pin, were inlaid with precious gemstones.

Ring of gold adorned with a pearl

Buddhist pilgrimage site
For centuries, Angkor's rulers prayed to Hindu gods, but in the late 13th century, Buddhism grew in importance. The site began to attract Buddhists from across Asia, as well as Zhou Daguan, a Chinese diplomat who wrote a book about Angkor.

Golden empire
The Khmer Empire was very wealthy. Its kings would wear a golden crown, bracelets around their wrists and ankles, and rings on fingers and toes. It was powerful, too—by the 12th century, the Khmers ruled a huge area of southeast Asia.

Buddhist pilgrims undertake long journeys for their spiritual development.

Nature takes over
In the 15th century, Angkor stopped being the capital of the Khmer Empire and the royals left. It was not abandoned, but fell into decline. Plants slowly grew over parts of the city.

Giant stone faces decorate the walls of the Bayon Temple in Angkor Thom.

Angkor Thom
In the late 12th century, King Jayavarman VII began building himself a new city complex within Angkor, calling it Angkor Thom. He kept some older temples within his city walls and built a few new ones, including the Bayon.

2 The inner temple was the most sacred place in Angkor Wat.

In this image, remains of dense villages that once surrounded the temple show up in a light orange color.

Shadows of a city
New technology has allowed archaeologists to see traces of ancient structures around Angkor Wat. Laser scanners were used to create maps of canals, roads, and villages.

A DAY IN ANGKOR WAT

King Suryavarman II is on his way to visit his temple. He crosses the sacred bridge, carried in a chair on his subjects' shoulders. The king is shaded by parasols but his priests and attendants must endure the full heat of the sun. Ordinary people and animals are not allowed on the bridge at all.

Royal builder
King Suryavarman II built Angkor Wat in the early 12th century. Constructing such a great Hindu temple showed his people and his enemies how powerful he was. His portrait is carved in one of the temple's friezes.

Village life
Large villages sprawled around the temple. Craftsmen and farmers lived here, and traded at markets for food, baskets, pots, and other things they needed.

This carving shows women trading fish at a market stall.

Rice grains

Growing rice
Rice was the main food in the Khmer Empire. People ate it every day, and used it to trade with. They dug complex systems of water channels, which allowed huge quantities of rice to be grown.

Sickle for cutting rice

Rice plant

Board games
To pass the time, many people played a board game that was similar to chess. Animal fights and sword swallowing were also popular forms of entertainment.

1 Lotus boats
Boats are used to harvest lotus flowers that will be used as offerings in the temple.

2 Procession
Two rows of royal attendants walk toward the temple, carrying offerings.

3 The king
King Suryavarman II is highly revered. He must be shaded by at least nine parasols.

"Those who caught a glimpse of the **king** were expected to **kneel** and **touch the earth** with their **brows**."

—Zhou Daguan, Chinese diplomat who visited Angkor in 1296

4 Worshippers
People fall to their knees and pray as the king is carried past them.

5 Hindu priests
A few temple priests, known as Brahmins, are walking along one of the shaded galleries.

6 Temple gate
On the other side of this grand gate is the sacred compound, with the temple at its center.

7 Elephant
This elephant is being trained to carry things. If it does well it might carry the king one day.

8 Food baskets
This man is laden with baskets full of rice from one of the nearby farms.

9 Cherished kids
Children are much loved in Angkor. They wear their long hair in a top knot, just like adults do.

CITY OF THE INCA

The city of Machu Picchu lay abandoned in the Andes Mountains for more than four hundred years, its location known only to a few local people. The hidden haven was built in the mid-15th century by a South American people called the Inca, who may have used it as a religious center or royal retreat.

The Inca Empire
The land controlled by the Inca ran along the mountainous western coast of South America. The Inca were highly organized and built a vast road network to connect their cities.

Khipu
The Inca didn't have a writing system. They recorded information using knotted strings called *khipus*. No one can read *khipu* today, which means most of what we know about the Inca comes from archaeology.

Inca emperor
The Inca leader was called the *Sapa Inca*. This *Sapa Inca* was called Pachacuti. Machu Picchu was one of his estates.

Hiram Bingham
In 1911, US explorer Hiram Bingham was in the Andes Mountains, searching for a lost city called Vilcabamba. Local people led him to Machu Picchu instead, and Bingham shared the story of the city with the rest of the world.

Excavating the city
In 1912, archaeologists began clearing the thick plants that had grown over Machu Picchu. They took thousands of photographs and uncovered artifacts that they took away to the US.

Machu Picchu today

Since Bingham first arrival and the excavations that followed, the site of the Inca city has been completely cleared of undergrowth, revealing buildings made of polished dry stone walls that have survived for hundreds of years. This stonework has been cleaned and patched, and some outlying structures have been completely rebuilt.

1 Sun stone

This stone was used as a sundial, with four points marking north, south, east, and west.

2 Houses

Inca homes were built with stone walls and thatched roofs.

Mountain top

The city sits on a mountain ridge, with steep cliffs dropping away all around it. The tallest mountain peak above the city, Huayna Picchu, was once topped by Inca temples.

1 **High priests**
This priest stands at the city's highest point, near a sacred stone that may have served as a calendar.

2 **Terrace view**
Nobles watching the emperor's ceremony enjoy the view from high-up terrace farms.

3 **Farming**
With little flat land around, farmers have cut stepped terrace fields into the slope.

4 **Procession**
Machu Picchu is home to many temples. These priests are on their way to one of them.

5 **Temple**
This is the city's main temple. It holds glittering golden images of Inti, the sun god.

6 **The emperor**
Every day the emperor comes here to sacrifice his warm woolen *uncu* (cloak) to Inti.

LIFE IN THE LOST CITY

It is a busy time of year at Machu Picchu. The emperor is visiting and he is in the middle of conducting a ceremony, closely watched by his high priests and nobles. At the same time, an envoy is carrying away an urgent message—what could it be?

7 Digging stone
Stone is being quarried so more structures can be built. Llamas help carry the heavy rock.

8 Envoy
This runner is off on an errand. He will blow his shell to warn people to get out of his way.

9 Khipu
A message has been knotted into this *khipu*. It must be something very important!

10 On guard!
In the grand main square, these royal guards are waiting for the emperor.

11 Storehouse
Goods from across the empire were kept in long, narrow storehouses.

12 Slow down!
This builder is angry—that envoy has gone by so fast that he has knocked down freshly-laid stone!

A HOLY CITY

Machu Picchu is a religious center. It has four temples, the most important of which is the Temple of the Sun, where the sun god Inti is worshipped. The Inca believed that the emperor was descended from Inti—perhaps that's why the royal family spends so much time in this holy city.

There are over **150 buildings** in the city of **Machu Picchu.**

Colorful clothing
The Inca used the wool of llamas, alpacas, and vicuñas to weave cloth. Their cloth was colorful, with beautiful, elaborate patterns. This is known because Inca textiles were preserved by the dry, cold climate of the Andes.

Geometric patterns decorate this tunic. The most valuable cloths were given as gifts or worn by high-status people.

This is a golden likeness of Inti, the sun god.

Temple
This sacred building has no roof and is open to the elements on one side. It was built from stones that were cut to fit perfectly, with no mortar needed to hold them together.

Mamakuna are women who sing and play drums at ceremonies. They are chosen as children and live in the temple while they are trained.

Music is an important part of Inca rituals. The instruments were usually played by women.

Brave soldiers sometimes receive rewards of gold from the emperor.

The Inca emperor only wears his *uncu* (a piece of clothing) once. Every day he burns the worn *uncu* in a special ceremony.

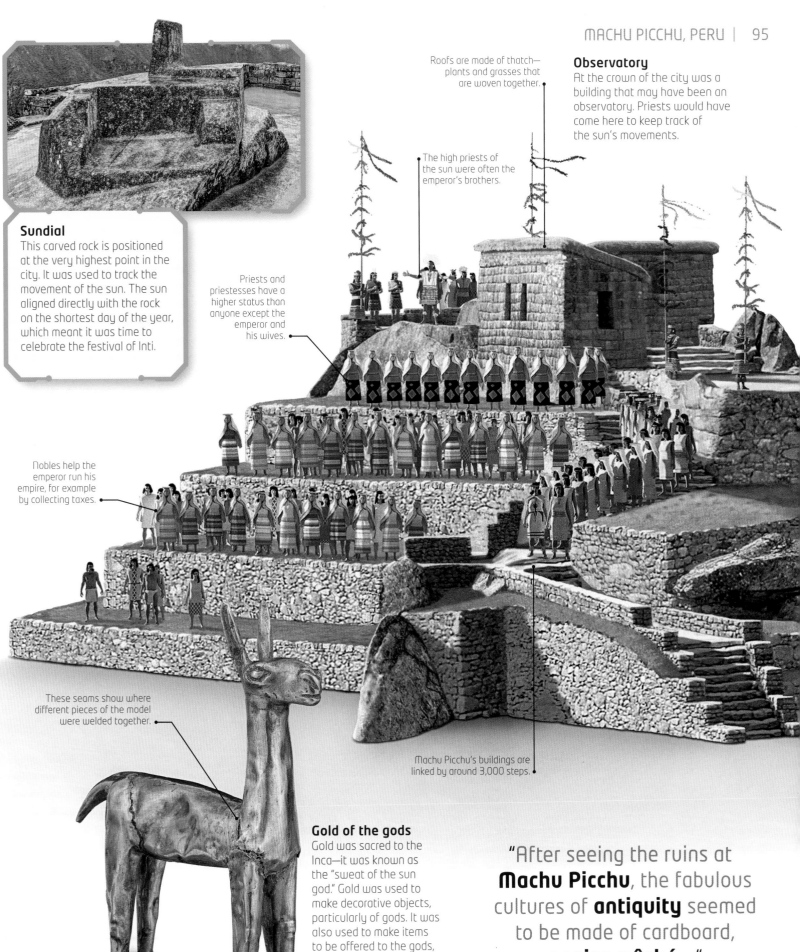

Sundial
This carved rock is positioned at the very highest point in the city. It was used to track the movement of the sun. The sun aligned directly with the rock on the shortest day of the year, which meant it was time to celebrate the festival of Inti.

Roofs are made of thatch— plants and grasses that are woven together.

Observatory
At the crown of the city was a building that may have been an observatory. Priests would have come here to keep track of the sun's movements.

The high priests of the sun were often the emperor's brothers.

Priests and priestesses have a higher status than anyone except the emperor and his wives.

Nobles help the emperor run his empire, for example by collecting taxes.

These seams show where different pieces of the model were welded together.

Machu Picchu's buildings are linked by around 3,000 steps.

Gold of the gods
Gold was sacred to the Inca—it was known as the "sweat of the sun god." Gold was used to make decorative objects, particularly of gods. It was also used to make items to be offered to the gods, such as this golden llama.

"After seeing the ruins at **Machu Picchu**, the fabulous cultures of **antiquity** seemed to be made of cardboard, **papier-mâché** ..."

—Pablo Neruda, Chilean poet (1904-1973)

INGENIOUS INCA

Machu Picchu is high up in the Andes Mountains. The air is thin here, and land is scarce. However, the Inca Empire is flourishing! A well-ordered society means that all goods are centrally organized and shared, and farmers have worked hard to find ways to grow as much food as possible.

Storehouse

Inca society was very organized. People had to work for the empire for part of the year and deliver what they produced to a local storehouse. Government officials then decided how the goods should be distributed.

People are bringing goods they have made to the storehouse.

Stone storehouses

Goods such as food, pottery, and metalwork were all kept inside the storehouses. To protect these valuable items, the storehouses had stone walls that still stand today, outliving the thatched roofs that kept the contents dry.

Inca pottery was decorated with intricate patterns.

Archaeologists have found more than **2,000 Inca storehouses** in South America.

Ceremonial drink

The Inca made an alcoholic drink from maize called *chicha*. People drank it and offered it to the gods. It was transported in two-handled vases, which could be tied to someone's back by using a rope between the handles. It was among the many things that were kept in the storehouses.

Terrace

Machu Picchu was surrounded by steep cliffs. This meant that not much land was available to grow food, and farms had to be built into the hillside.

Most Inca people are farmers, craftsmen, or servants.

Stone walls absorbed the sun's heat in the day, which helped keep the plants warm at night.

The flat areas formed by the terrace provided space for different crops to be planted together—beans could climb up the stalks of maize, with squash growing underneath.

DIGGING THE SOIL

Inca farmers used a device called a *chakitacclla* to help them plant seeds. This was a long wooden stick that had a curving handle and foot rest tied to it. The *chakitacclla* made it easy for the farmers to dig holes in the earth using the pressure from their feet and their own body weight.

Farms

When viewed from above it is possible to see how the Inca dug steps into the hillside and built walls to keep the vertical parts upright. These slivers of flat land are known as terraces. Inca farmers used them to grow food including maize, which was also turned into *chicha*.

WORKING ANIMALS

Llamas are native to South America. The Inca farmed these animals for their meat, milk, and wool. They also used llamas as pack animals to carry heavy loads along mountain trails. Many llamas still live in the Andes Mountains near the ruins of Machu Picchu today.

THE SILK ROAD

The 16th-century caravansary (inn) of Izadkhast sits alongside an ancient trading route winding through the hot, dusty Iranian desert. It was one of many outposts constructed to protect merchants traveling between Asia and Europe. Dotted along the road, caravansaries offered travelers a secure roof for the night, as well as a place for people to exchange goods, skills, customs, and ideas.

Controlling trade

Izadkhast is in Iran (previously known as Persia), between Europe and China. Traders on the Silk Road had to pass through the region, allowing the Safavid Empire that ruled the area to grow rich selling goods to traveling merchants.

Imposing Izadkhast

The arched gateway was the only way in or out of the caravansary and would have been locked at night to keep the guests safe. The courtyard was a place for trade and socializing, while the niches around the edge provided merchants and their servants with a private space to rest. This caravansary was part of a group of buildings, including a castle.

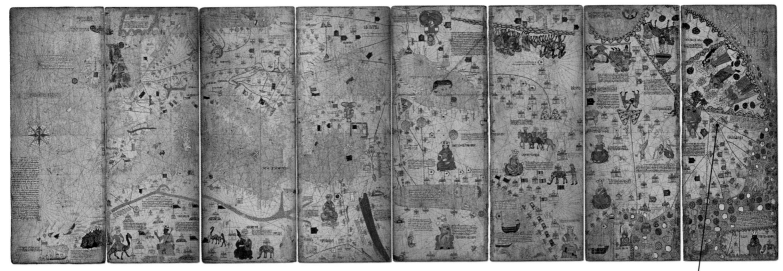

The Silk Road
This Spanish map shows the areas connected by the Silk Road, the network of trade routes between China and Europe. The mapmakers may have used the reports of traders such as Marco Polo to help them complete their work.

Beijing in China is described on the map as the city of the great Khan.

A dangerous journey
Travelers along the Silk Road often joined large groups called caravans. Together, these traders were better able to survive extreme desert conditions and protect themselves from bandit attacks.

Rest stops
Caravansaries were places where long-distance travelers could break their journeys. They were built next to busy trade routes, around a day's journey apart. As this photo from around 1898 shows, caravansaries continued to be used for hundreds of years.

Shah Abbas
The best-known ruler of the Persian Safavid Empire is Shah Abbas the Great, who ruled from 1588 to 1629. Under his rule, Persia was a strong military empire. Art flourished, trade links were strengthened, and many caravansaries, including Izadkhast, were built.

Rich silks would have been imported from China.

Niches provided shade from the desert sun.

This type of curved sword is called a scimitar.

1 Preparing food
The women of the caravansary cook in a separate area, away from the male travelers.

2 Refreshments
A server brings drinks to a group of merchants who have all come from different places.

3 Fun and games
This traveler has agreed to play whoever wins the current game of *shatranj*.

4 Beast of burden
Camels, a valuable form of transportation, must be stabled before the humans can rest.

5 Haggling
Not missing a chance to trade, these travelers argue over the price of some fine carpets.

6 Late arrival
A newcomer arrives at the caravansary. He has made it just before the gates are locked.

A BUSY EVENING

It is dusk at Izadkhast and the light is fading fast. Tired travelers are settling in, sheltering from the cold and unknown dangers of the desert. People have come from all over Asia, Africa, and Europe. They cook, eat, stable their animals, and organize their wares before going to bed, ahead of another long day's travel tomorrow.

This figurine is loaded with Chinese pottery.

Ships of the desert
Along the deserts of the Silk Road, camels were the best form of transportation. They are strong, able to carry heavy loads of up to 496 lb (225 kg). Camels also cope well in dry conditions—they need much less water than horses, and their wide hooves stop them from sinking into the sand.

This jacket was made of metal-wrapped silk and silver foil.

Valuable silks
Silk thread is made from the cocoon of a particular species of moth. It can be woven into a soft, light, luxurious fabric. For a long time, silk production was a closely guarded Chinese secret. Its scarcity made it extremely valuable, while the beauty of the cloth meant it was desired by all who saw it.

The detail of the braid shows the skill of the Persian tailor who made the jacket.

Fine metalwork
Exquisitely crafted metal goods were traded all along the Silk Road. This candlestick was made in the Safavid era. It is made from bronze—a mixture of copper and other metals.

7 Evening prayers
Over by the fountain, a Muslim traveler kneels on a mat to begin his sunset prayer.

8 Silk for sale
A merchant's servant shakes the dust from a piece of silk his master wishes to sell.

The game of *shatranj*
It was not just goods that were traded along the Silk Road. The Indian game *chaturanga* traveled to Persia, where it developed into a game called *shatranj*, which eventually became chess.

These *shatranj* pieces are simpler versions of the chess figures we use today.

THE ISLAND OF RAPA NUI

On an island in the middle of the Pacific Ocean, around 900 monumental statues called *moai* dominate the landscape. This island is Rapa Nui, also known as Easter Island because its first European visitor arrived on Easter Sunday in 1722. The statues were erected between 800 and 1200 CE by Polynesian people. By the late 18th century, most of the statues had been toppled. Work to reerect them began in 1960.

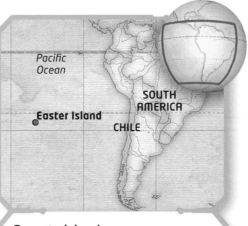

Pacific Ocean

Easter Island

SOUTH AMERICA

CHILE

Remote island
The island of Rapa Nui is one of the most isolated in Polynesia, a group of 1,000 islands in the Pacific Ocean. Rapa Nui is part of Chile, which is more than 2,175 miles (3,500 km) away.

Giants of Rapa Nui
The colossal *moai* statues that dot Rapa Nui were thought to represent spirits of important ancestors. They faced inland to watch over and protect the islanders. Most of the statues are 13 ft (4 m) high but some are as tall as 33 ft (10 m). Some stand alone, others are arranged in lines.

Discovering the eye
In 1978, archaeologists found pieces of white coral while excavating a *moai*. They realized it had to be an eye when it fitted into the *moai's* eye socket. This eye—the only original one—is on display in the Sebastián Englert Museum on Rapa Nui.

This end of the paddle represents a face, with earrings on either side.

Dance paddle
Dance ceremonies were an important part of Rapa Nui culture. During dances, both men and women wielded pairs of dance paddles called *rapa*. The *rapa* were spun on axes carried by the dancers.

This end of the paddle represents a person's body.

Lost language
A writing system has been found at Rapa Nui, carved into pieces of wood. It is called *rongorongo* and features hundreds of pictograms of birds and animals, laid out in ordered lines. So far, no one has been able to decipher it.

Pictograms were carved into the wood using shark teeth or sharp pieces of obsidian rock.

Canoes
The Polynesians were expert ship builders, navigators, and sailors. They made voyages of thousands of miles around the Pacific Ocean in wooden canoes. Today the people of Rapa Nui honor this tradition by racing in reed canoes.

Wooden carvings
The islanders of Rapa Nui did not just work in stone. Finely-carved wooden statues called *moai kavakava* depict men so thin that their ribs are showing. It is thought that these statues were kept in people's homes on the island.

Many of the *moai* at Rapa Nui sit on long ceremonial platforms called *ahu*.

A volcanic island
Rapa Nui formed when volcanoes erupted, and the lava they threw out hardened into rock. Three now-extinct volcanoes dominate the landscape: Poike, Rano Kau, and Terevaka.

1 Team work
The statues are heavy, so teams of people work together to pull them into place.

2 Eye sockets
The rope is tied around the *moai*'s eye sockets. Detailed eyes will be added later.

3 Strong features
The *moai*'s head is large in comparison to its body. Its face is carved with strong, stylized features.

4 Body art
Elaborate tattoos and painted patterns decorate the bodies of the islanders.

5 Grass clothing
It's warm on Rapa Nui. The islanders wear grass loincloths to help them stay cool.

6 Ramp
This statue must make its way up a ramp onto the *ahu* (ceremonial platform).

The giant statues at Rapa Nui weigh an average of 14 tons.

ERECTING THE MOAI

The islanders of Rapa Nui have one more *moai* to erect. They have already transported the statue across the island, using ropes to rock it from side to side to inch it forward, without lifting it off the ground. Now, they are straining to hoist it into position beside a row of finished *moai*. It's hot and heavy work!

The quarry
Around 95 percent of the *moai* were carved in Rano Raraku quarry, from a porous volcanic rock called tuff. Each statue was made from a huge single piece of tuff. Nearly 400 *moai* statues still lie in the quarries where they were carved.

Complex carving
The *moais'* backs are decorated with figures called petroglyphs. The heads and fronts of the statues were carved as they lay on the ground, but their backs were finished after the statues had been lifted upright.

The canoe is a symbol of the carver's family.

Red *pukao*, or topknot

Red topknots
Some of the *moai* have a red *pukao*, or topknot. The *pukaos* are made from red scoria, a different rock from the tuff used for the bodies. The *moai* with *pukaos* are thought to be among the later statues carved.

Sweet potato payments
To obtain a statue, people would give a carver sweet potatoes, chickens, and tools. Sweet potatoes are originally from South America. The Polynesians would have sailed thousands of miles across the Pacific Ocean in order to bring the crop to Rapa Nui.

7 Carved backs
Patterns and animal- and birdlike figures are carved into the backs of each of the *moai* statues.

8 Volcanic rock
Rano Raraku crater, the source of the *moai* tuff, towers over the islanders as they work.

EYES OF THE MOAI
The bright white eyes of the Moai statues on the island of Rapa Nui are carved from white coral stone. The pupil is made from red scoria stone. The Moai's creators added the eyes when the rest of the statue was finished. This is the only Moai to have had its eyes restored.

110 | TAKEDA, JAPAN

JAPANESE FORTRESS

Perched above a sea of clouds, the ruins of Takeda Castle hug the contours of their hilltop home. This mountain fortress was first built in 1441, then had immense stone walls built to improve its defenses in about 1585. These alterations were made during a period of civil unrest when castles were being built and strengthened across Japan.

Strategic location
Takeda Castle is in the west of Honshu, Japan's central island. It sits on a mountain ridge 1,158 ft (353 m) above sea level, overlooking a highway.

Organized society
Japan had a class-based system. Groups of people such as warriors, farmers, artisans, and merchants were clearly separate, with strict rules on what each group could do. At the top of society were lords called *daimyo*, served by samurai warriors.

Superb structures
Most Japanese castles had some features in common: a central keep; several courtyards; then walls, watchtowers, and ditches. This is Himeji Castle, which has been restored to look as it did in its prime.

This *daimyo* is too important to walk—he is being carried in the middle of a group of his retainers.

Battle flags
Daimyo led armies of samurai on the battlefield. Each *daimyo* had his own standard. As the selection below shows, these could be flags, fans, or helmets. Displayed on a tall pole, standards showed which *daimyo* were present at a battle.

Inside the castle
The rooms in the castle's keep were comfortably furnished with paper walls and soft floor mats. *Daimyo* showed off their wealth by decorating their rooms with the finest paintings, such as the one on the back wall of this reconstructed room.

Courtyard complex

Takeda Castle is built around a succession of courtyards, each of which an attacker would have to fight through. The central courtyard in the foreground is where the *daimyo* and his family would have had their living quarters.

The castle's walls were so thickly built that they still stand, more than 400 years since it was abandoned.

Natural defenses

Takeda Castle is positioned on an isolated mountaintop, which gave it a strong defensive position. Abandoned in 1600, its central buildings have crumbled away over time, leaving just the impressive stone walls. Despite being in ruins, the castle's remains still make for an imposing structure today.

The castle's location is so high that it sometimes sits above the clouds.

Civil strife

In the 16th century, Japan suffered a century-long period of civil war, with its *daimyo* fighting each other in attempts to gain land and power. Many built castles to defend themselves. One of the last clashes of the era was the Battle of Sekigahara, shown here.

There are **more than 100** castles in **Japan** today. Only **12** still have their **original keep.**

1 The lady
The *daimyo's* wife is on the balcony. She points her husband's arrival out to their son.

2 Servants
Attendants surround the lady of the castle, ready to take any order she may give.

3 Son and heir
The *daimyo's* son cannot wait to join his father on hunting trips when he is older.

4 Home again
The *daimyo* has returned! He is hot and tired after his journey home.

5 Samurai guard
Loyal samurai guards stay near the *daimyo* at all times He is never alone.

6 Yagura
These turrets are used as watchtowers. They provide a good view of the surrounding land.

THE DAIMYO RETURNS

The *daimyo* is coming back from a successful hunting trip in the mountains. He rides his horse into an inner courtyard, while the castle's residents gather to watch their lord's return.

Castle gardens
Japanese castles had elaborate, carefully planted gardens with bridges, tea houses, and rare plants. They were designed to be admired from the keep as well as walked around. This garden is at Osaka Castle.

These flasks are made from wood. They are decorated with gold and layers of a hard paint called lacquer.

Sake flasks
These ornamental flasks contain *sake*, an alcoholic drink made from fermented rice. It was only drunk on special occasions. It was also offered to the gods at New Year and at religious festivals.

Samurai armor
The samurai were highly-trained soldiers, who learned swordsmanship and archery from a young age. They swore loyalty to their *daimyo*. Samurai armor was decorated with fearsome designs including dragons and snarling faces.

Horses carrying samurai wore their own armor, such as this mask.

Noble ladies
Japanese women were trained in many things including calligraphy, poetry, music, and dance. When the *daimyo* was away, his wife, the lady of the castle, was in charge of the fortress' defenses.

7 Masugata
This courtyard between the castle's main and second gates forms an easily defensible space.

8 Peasants
These peasants are carrying rice, which they will pay as tax to the *daimyo*.

THE GREAT WALL OF CHINA

The Great Wall is the name given to the vast system of fortifications and walls snaking across 8,000 miles (13,000 km) of northern China. It was designed to protect China from its enemies to the north, especially the Mongols. The part of the Wall shown here, called the Mutianyu section, was completed in 1572. It looks almost the same now as when it was built 450 years ago.

The Wall was us[...] built on the stee[...] part of a hill, to [...] extra difficult to [...]

Protecting the capital
Mutianyu is in a hilly part of northeast China. It is just 43 miles (70 km) from the Chinese capital, Beijing, so was one of the Wall's most important sections.

Food and drink
Soldiers on the Great Wall ate simple food such as rice and vegetables, brought in from nearby farms and villages. To drink, troops were given dried blocks of tea leaves known as *Bing cha* ("tea bread"). Fresh water was not always safe to drink, as it could contain bacteria, so it was best to boil it first and drink it hot with tea.

Strong stone walls
Known as ramparts, the brick walls at Mutianyu were 30 ft (9 m) high and 13–16 ft (4–5 m) across. The tops of the wall had sections cut out called crenellations through which cannons could be fired.

As well as cannons, spiked "rollers" were dropped over the side of the Wall to stop people climbing up. They were also rolled along the floor to trip-up (and seriously injure) attackers.

General in charge
Work began on the Great Wall around 221 BCE, but it was quite a simple and low structure at first. After a Mongol attack on China in 1550, the general Qi Jiguang was asked to strengthen the Wall, adding the watchtowers and defensive ramparts we see today at places such as Mutianyu.

Seal of approval
Builders had to stamp each batch of bricks so the authorities could find and punish them if the bricks were poor-quality. Many of those bricks can still be seen today.

When the enemy was spotted, piles of sticks and wood were set alight on top of these watch towers. The "wolf smoke" they gave off could be seen for miles. It was called wolf smoke because wolves were seen as a sign of danger in China.

The hut on the guard tower roof provided cover from bad weather and extra storage space for food and weapons.

A vast construction

The Wall that is visible today was mainly built during the Ming Dynasty (1368-1644), with most work happening in the mid-1500s. Parts of the Wall have been carefully restored, such as this section at Mutianyu.

The "Wild Wall"

Some sections of the Wall, like Jiankou, close to Mutianyu, are in a very poor state of repair. Today these crumbling areas are called the "Wild Wall."

Secret ingredient

Until very recently, scientists wondered why the mortar holding the bricks of the Wall had lasted so long and remained so strong. Tests have now shown that the mortar cement of limestone and sand had a secret ingredient that made it super-strong: ground-up sticky rice. Also called glutinous rice, it actually gets harder the older it gets.

DEFEND THE WALL!

Builders are putting the finishing touches on a new guard tower, and some of the sentries are almost dozing off when suddenly a warning cry rings out: "Raiders!" Mongol troops are launching a daring attack and the Chinese soldiers must scramble to fight them off.

1 Forest
These trees give cover to approaching attackers. But the trees next to the Wall have been cut down.

2 Watch out!
An eagle-eyed soldier in the guard tower sees the enemy coming and raises the alarm.

3 Raiders
The Mongols, from the region north of the Great Wall, were China's most dangerous foes.

4 Crossing over
The Mongols cleverly use ladders laid flat to cross the deep trenches in front of the Wall.

5 Surprise attack!
Very sharp Mongol swords can easily cut through the guard's protective armor.

6 Guard tower
The "command center" of each section of the Wall houses food, weapons, and armor.

7 Construction
Builders finish work on a new tower that will make the Wall easier to defend in future.

8 Cannon
This gun fires cannonballs that are hollow and filled with explosive gun power.

9 Beacon
Warning smoke lets troops further along the Wall know that the Mongols are here.

10 Patrolman
This solider brings word of an attack on another section of the Wall. The raid is worse than feared!

11 Terrace farms
People at the nearby farm are not scared. They know the Wall will protect them.

12 Brick kilns
Bricks for the new tower are made on site inside kilns where it can get as hot as 1,470°F (800°C).

Rainproof roof
Tiles helped seal and protect tower roofs from rain. They were decorated at the roof ends with animals, plants, symbols, or even a *gao tie* ("monster face") which was meant to scare off evil spirits.

TOUGH TOWERS

Guard towers on the Wall are sturdily built and some have small, roofed buildings on top called *pufang*, or sentry posts. Both the tower and the *pufang* are used as shelter and for storing food, water, armor, weapons, and other supplies.

Crossbow
Chinese people used crossbows for around 2,000 years. Smaller ones, like this example, were used to defend city walls, and larger versions were used on the Great Wall.

A small crossbow's range is 100–130 ft (30–40 m).

Explosive ammunition
Each tower had a good supply of cannonballs. Although they look solid, each iron ball was hollow and filled with gunpowder, causing the ball to explode when it hit the ground.

Carved creatures called roof guardians were said to bring good luck.

Rice is a staple of the guards' diet, so there is always lots of it in storage.

The *pufang* sits directly in the middle of the tower roof.

Stone for the tower's bricks was all mined from hills nearby.

Crossbows are stored in the tower and only used when an attack takes place.

The largest towers have stone or brick floors, which makes them easy to keep clean and dry. Smaller towers have floors made of earth.

Although some towers have stone or brick stairs between each level, this one just has a bamboo ladder. This makes it hard to carry heavy loads up and down.

"There in the mist, **enormous, majestic, silent, and terrible,** stood the **Great Wall of China** ..."

—W. Somerset Maugham, author (1874-1965)

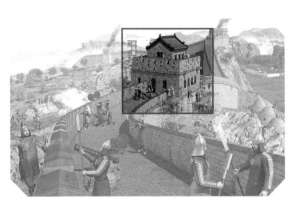

It rains a lot in China, so roofs always hang out a long way over walls, to protect them from dampness.

These openings are known as loopholes. Guards can drop rocks and grenades or fire arrows from them.

The Ming Wall and towers were mostly built by the guards themselves, with some help from skilled builders and craftsmen.

MONGOL ATTACKERS

The Great Wall was built to defend China from attacks by the Mongols. Under Genghis Khan the Mongols had conquered much of Asia and parts of Europe in the 1200s. By the 1500s they were less powerful, but still fearsome warriors, famed for their horse-riding and archery skills.

Windows give ventilation to stop the food inside the tower going moldy or gunpowder getting damp. A walled corridor helps keep things dry when it rains.

"Reclining moon" glaives have long, curving blades.

Triple-bladed pole-arms like this are called halberds.

Weapons of war

Each tower held a collection of swords, called *jian*; spears; and long, stabbing weapons called pole-arms or glaives. They came in all shapes and sizes but all had the same purpose: to allow the user to fight their enemy from a safe distance.

Barrels of gunpowder are kept locked in the tower because it is such a valuable and dangerous substance.

VILLAGE LIFE

Soldiers and their families live in villages next to the Wall, with troops heading there when it was their turn to do guard duty. Farmers liked being close to the Wall as they could sell their produce to the troops. Farm and village houses were both usually based around an enclosed "courtyard" design.

House roofs are plain, without the carved roof guardians seen on temples and Great Wall guard towers.

The roof overhangs the courtyard to provide shade in summertime

Ancestor worship
Most Chinese houses, had an altar or shrine where incense was burned, and gifts and offerings were left to honor dead family members. This is known as ancestor worship and many Chinese people still practice it today.

Animal pens made from local wood or bamboo

Animal helpers
Farmers used donkeys to move heavy loads in wicker or straw baskets strapped to their sides. Donkeys are still seen today, working hard on the steep hills near the Great Wall where cars and trucks cannot go.

The outside walls have no windows. This gives the house privacy and security.

This medium-size pen is for donkeys. They spend their days working, so for them the pen is a place to rest.

"**I dig the well** from which I drink. I farm the soil which yields my food. **I share creation**. Kings can do no more."

—Traditional Chinese proverb

The pen for goats is the largest outdoor part of the farm.

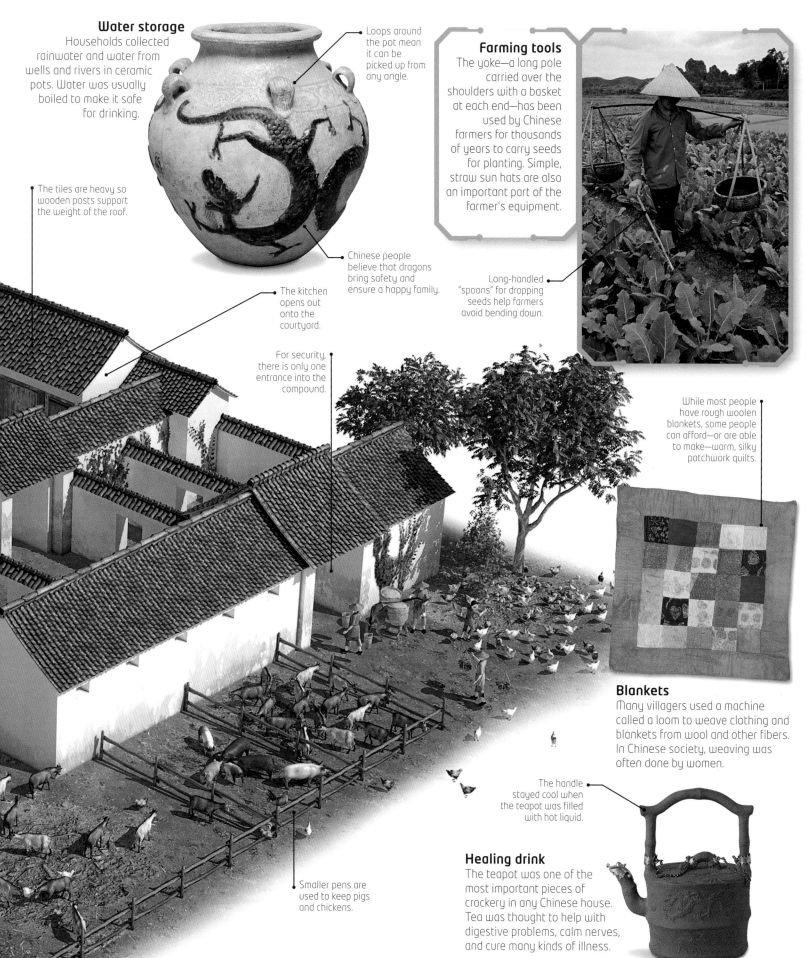

Water storage
Households collected rainwater and water from wells and rivers in ceramic pots. Water was usually boiled to make it safe for drinking.

Loops around the pot mean it can be picked up from any angle.

Farming tools
The yoke—a long pole carried over the shoulders with a basket at each end—has been used by Chinese farmers for thousands of years to carry seeds for planting. Simple, straw sun hats are also an important part of the farmer's equipment.

The tiles are heavy so wooden posts support the weight of the roof.

Chinese people believe that dragons bring safety and ensure a happy family.

The kitchen opens out onto the courtyard.

Long-handled "spoons" for dropping seeds help farmers avoid bending down.

For security, there is only one entrance into the compound.

While most people have rough woolen blankets, some people can afford—or are able to make—warm, silky patchwork quilts.

Blankets
Many villagers used a machine called a loom to weave clothing and blankets from wool and other fibers. In Chinese society, weaving was often done by women.

The handle stayed cool when the teapot was filled with hot liquid.

Smaller pens are used to keep pigs and chickens.

Healing drink
The teapot was one of the most important pieces of crockery in any Chinese house. Tea was thought to help with digestive problems, calm nerves, and cure many kinds of illness.

PIRATE SHIP

On a dark, stormy night in 1717, a pirate ship hit a sandbank and sank to the bottom of the sea, taking with it all its treasure and most of the crew. This unlucky ship was the *Whydah*. The wreck site, off the Atlantic coast of the US, is the first ever proven to be that of a pirate ship.

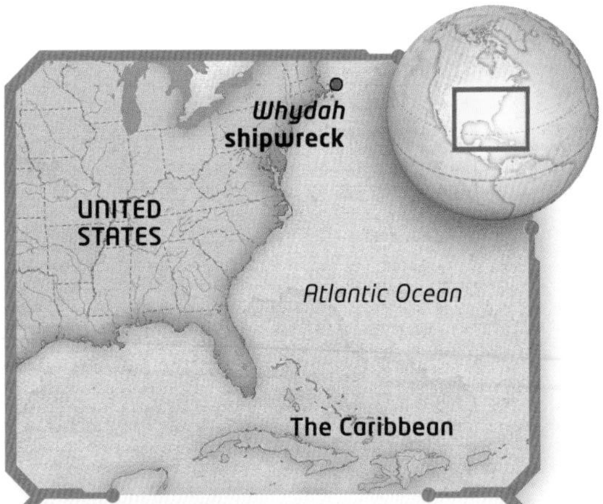

Changing fates

The *Whydah*, seen here as a model, was an English slave ship. Setting out from the Caribbean, loaded with takings from the sale of enslaved Africans, the ship was seized by pirates. Their leader, "Black Sam" Bellamy, transferred treasure and guns from ships he'd looted earlier to the *Whydah*, and sailed her north toward the US.

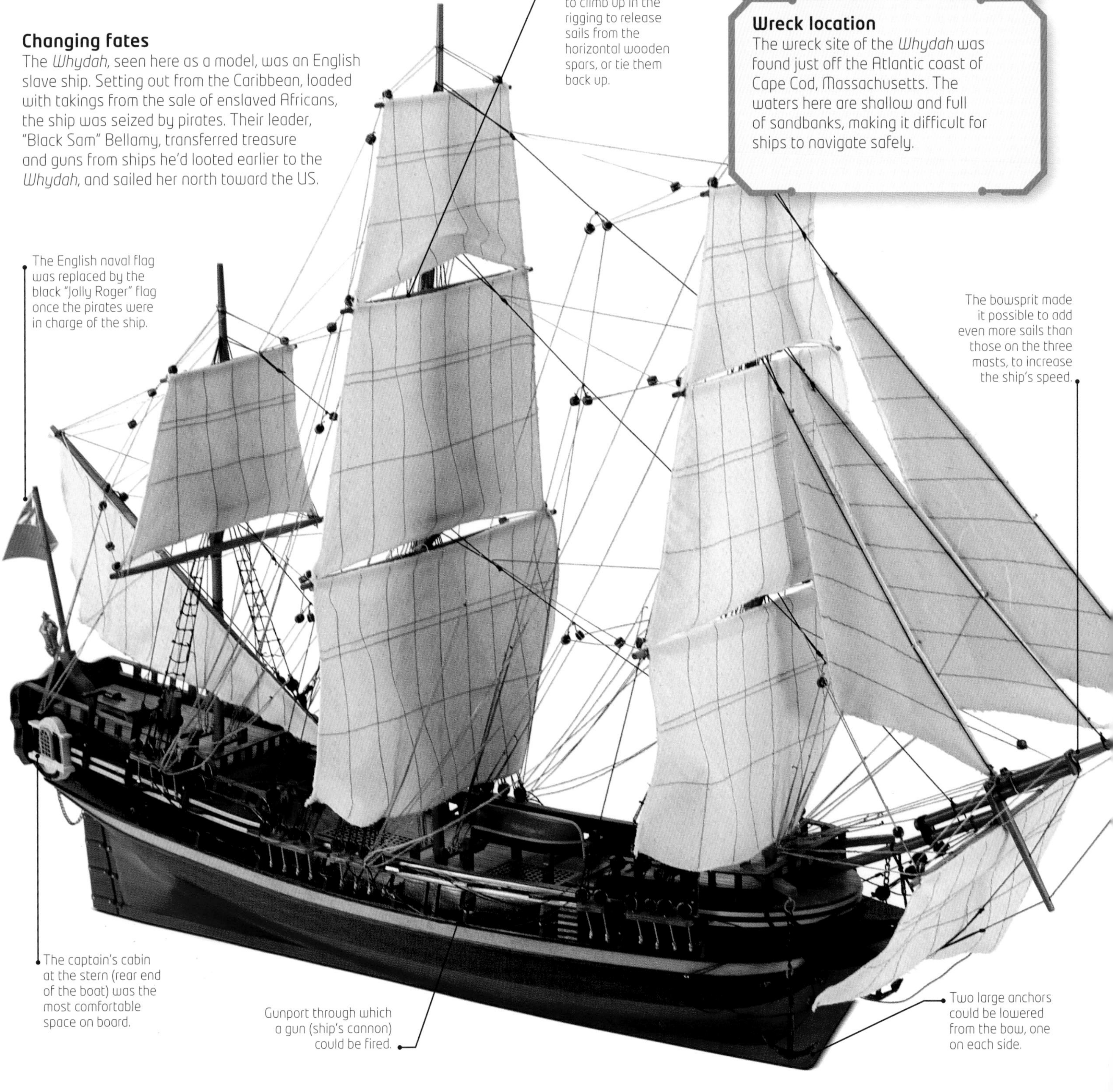

Whydah shipwreck

United States

Atlantic Ocean

The Caribbean

Wreck location

The wreck site of the *Whydah* was found just off the Atlantic coast of Cape Cod, Massachusetts. The waters here are shallow and full of sandbanks, making it difficult for ships to navigate safely.

Crew members had to climb up in the rigging to release sails from the horizontal wooden spars, or tie them back up.

The English naval flag was replaced by the black "Jolly Roger" flag once the pirates were in charge of the ship.

The bowsprit made it possible to add even more sails than those on the three masts, to increase the ship's speed.

The captain's cabin at the stern (rear end of the boat) was the most comfortable space on board.

Gunport through which a gun (ship's cannon) could be fired.

Two large anchors could be lowered from the bow, one on each side.

Marking the spot
In 1717, as news of the *Whydah's* sinking spread, the governor of Massachusetts sent Captain Cyprian Southack to collect any valuables he could find. Southack couldn't salvage anything, but he did mark the wreck location on a map.

Notes on the map say where the ship was lost, and that 102 men drowned.

Archaeologist at work
The *Whydah* wreck site is still being explored by teams of divers. All finds are taken to a laboratory, where they are painstakingly excavated by expert archaeologists.

Archaeologists work slowly and delicately, to avoid damaging the artifacts.

Copper bracelets such as these, found at the wreck site, were used to pay for enslaved people in Africa.

Piracy and the slave trade
Pirates often came across ships involved in the transatlantic slave trade, in which enslaved Africans were taken to, and sold in, the Americas. Many pirates were Black—some joined pirate crews after escaping slavery, and others when the slave ships they were held on were seized.

Hidden treasure
Objects buried in the sandy seafloor end up encased in hard clumps called concretions. These form when iron reacts with salts in the water. They are soaked in freshwater tanks to preserve the items inside until these can be excavated, by hand or chemically.

A coin that has been hidden from view for over 300 years is revealed.

This ring and Spanish coins were found at the *Whydah* wreck site.

Pirate gold
Spanish galleons constantly crossed the Atlantic Ocean, carrying gold and silver from the Americas to Europe. Spanish coins were used as currency all over the world and often ended up in pirate treasure troves.

The *Whydah's* bell has writing around the top that says "Whydah Gally 1716".

Treasure hunt
Stirred by tales of the sinking, and the 1717 map, diver Barry Clifford set out to find the *Whydah*. In 1984, he found the wreck site after 15 years of searching. The ship had rotted away, but he found coins and guns, and then the ship's bell. The bell's inscription confirmed that the wreck was definitely that of the *Whydah*.

The ship's bell was made of bronze. Struck every half hour, it helped sailors keep track of when their watch began and ended.

1 Hold tight!
High up in the rigging, members of the crew are blown around by the roaring winds.

2 Carpenter
Thomas Davies, the carpenter, is frantically making repairs to the ship.

3 The captain
Captain Bellamy shouts out orders to his crew, but it's hard to hear him over the storm.

4 At the wheel
The pilot, 16-year-old John Julian, is a skilled sailor but struggles to keep the ship on course.

5 Seasick
Constant rocking has made this seaman sick. He clings tightly to the ship's side.

6 Boy overboard
Boy pirate John King is flung overboard, followed shortly after by a weighty gun.

PIRATES IN PERIL

It is after midnight, and the *Whydah* is caught in the throes of a raging tempest. Captain Bellamy and his crew work at a frenzied pace to fight the storm, but it is fierce, and the ship is heavily laden. In a terrible moment, the *Whydah* hits a sandbank below the water and begins to topple over. These are the *Whydah*'s last minutes, and all but two men will go down with their ship.

The crew struggle to hold on as they pull in the ship's sails.

Life on board

All crew members were treated equally, but fresh food was hard to come by. Pirates would eat whatever they could catch or take from passing ships—and the *Whydah* had a stove and a well-used teapot.

The *Whydah*'s teapot probably got its dent before the shipwreck.

Loaded ship

The *Whydah* was heavily loaded when it sank—full of large iron cannons, which would have helped drag it down. On board a ship, cannons are referred to as "guns."

More than 50 guns have been salvaged.

Pirate style

Most pirates wore clothes that were comfortable and practical for life at sea. But they also obtained more decorative and luxurious clothes from looted ships. They sometimes wore these items to show off.

Tiny pirate

Not all pirates were adults. Around 9 years old, John King chose to join Bellamy's crew when they attacked the ship he was on. But his pirate career was short—a child's leg bone, silk stocking, and shoe were found beneath a gun at the wreck site.

One of John King's leather shoes

Gold buttons and fine belt buckles discovered at the wreck site

"I am a **free prince**, and I have as much authority to **make war** on the whole world, as he who has a **hundred sail** of ships ..."

—Captain Sam Bellamy of the *Whydah* (1689-1717)

7 **Loose guns**
The guns have come loose. They roll across the deck, then plunge into the water.

8 **Flag down**
The mast snaps and falls, carrying the pirate flag down into the sea below.

BOOM TOWN

In 1859, a man called W. S. Bodey found gold in a remote part of California. Before he could exploit his discovery, Bodey froze to death in a blizzard, but the news of the gold spread. People flocked to the area seeking jobs, and the town of Bodie was born. By 1880, its population had reached 7,000. But as the gold ran out most of the inhabitants left, and today Bodie is a ghost town.

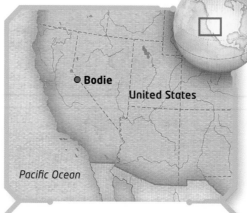

The American West
Bodie lies 8,375 ft (2,553 m) up in the Sierra Nevada mountains, in Mono County, California. The area is dusty and dry, hot in summer and freezing in winter.

The Standard Mill
The biggest building in Bodie today is known as the Standard Mill. It took material dug up by miners and separated the gold and silver in it from less valuable minerals. This industrial process caused much environmental damage.

Fighting fires
As Bodie was a town built mostly of wood, fires were a constant concern. At one time it had four separate fire companies, with carriages loaded with water pumps that were operated by hand.

This pipe could attach via a flexible hose to one of the fire hydrants installed on Bodie's streets in 1880.

This T-shaped shaft allowed the wagon to be pulled by horses or by men holding onto the bar.

Bodie's jail was small and only had two cells.

Keeping the streets safe
Law enforcement in Bodie was the responsibility of John F. Kirgan, the town's jailer and constable. Fights, shootings, and stabbings sometimes took place in the town, but Kirgan and his team worked hard to keep the peace.

A ghost town
Bodie's last residents left in the 1960s, leaving their possessions behind. Today, the buildings are preserved in a form of "arrested decay." This means that no one is allowed to move anything in any of the houses.

A glimpse of the past

From 1881, Bodie's population began to decline as people moved away. By 1915, most of the townsfolk had left, and in 1962 the now almost deserted town was declared a California State Historic Park. This means that the 100 or so buildings still standing today give unique insights into the lives of the people who had been living there.

1 The Dechambeau Hotel is one of Bodie's few brick-built buildings. In 1880 it served as the town's post office.

2 Bodie's busiest road, Main Street, going left to right, meets Green Street, running up and down, at this intersection.

3 This building was once Bodie's schoolhouse. Pupils were taught here until 1942. The original desks still stand in rows inside.

Immigrants from Asia

Several hundred Chinese people lived in Bodie, in an area known as "Chinatown." Many ran mule trains—packs of mules that carried in the wood used to heat Bodie's stoves.

A BUSY DAY IN BODIE

It's another hot afternoon in the summer of 1880 as the citizens of Bodie go about their business on Main Street. It seems as though every day brings change as people seeking to profit from the mining of gold arrive from out of town and set up new homes and businesses. Bodie is booming.

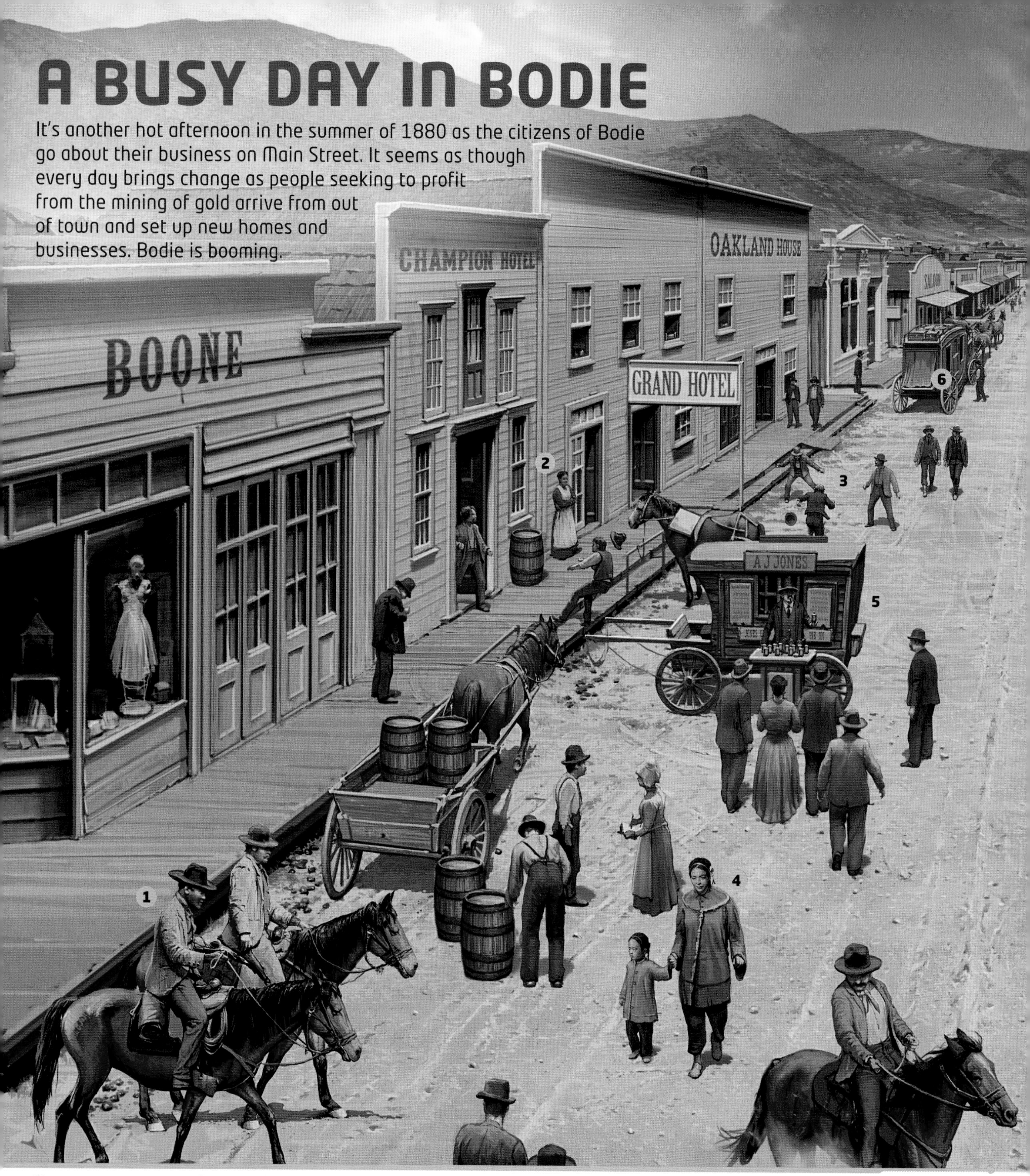

BOONE

CHAMPION HOTEL

OAKLAND HOUSE

GRAND HOTEL

SALOON

A.J. JONES

1 New arrivals
These men are visiting from a nearby ranch. They need to find a stable for their horses.

2 Hairdresser
Jane Carter, one of the town's hairdressers, is taking a break between customers.

3 Bar fight
A brawl at one of the saloons has spilled into the street, attracting a pair of lawmen.

4 Shopping trip
This mother and child are off to Boone's store to pick up some supplies and maybe a toy.

5 Traveling doctor
A crowd has gathered to see what this healer has to offer before he moves on to the next town.

6 Precious cargo
The coach is loading up with gold and silver bullion. It is protected by an armed guard.

7 Bodie burning?
The firehouse crew are scrambling to respond to a call about a fire in the north end of town.

8 The stamp mill
Smoke billows out of the stamp mill as it processes the ore dug up from the mines.

9 Mule train
There are few trees near town so firewood is brought from far away by teams of mules.

10 Tag!
School is done for the day and a couple kids are playing in the street on the way home.

11 Freight delivery
This massive wagon brings supplies from out of town. It is so heavy it takes 16 mules to pull it.

12 Whoa, girl!
A young horse is startled by all the noise in town. Her rider is doing his best to calm her.

BOONE'S STORE

The general store is one of the most important shops in any small town. Bodie has several, of which Boone's on Main Street survived for the longest time. Inside, the store stocks food, clothing, toys, tools, and much more. All these crucial goods come into town on the wagons that drive along the road running through the canyon to the north of the town.

Prominent position

Boone's had a good location on Bodie's Main Street. It was named after the store's owner, Harvey Boone, who opened his doors in 1879. Boone owned several other businesses and was considered one of Bodie's leading citizens. He was also a relative of the famous explorer Daniel Boone.

Durable clothing

Jeans were invented in 1873 in the US and quickly became popular as work clothes. Most of the miners in Bodie would have worn jeans like this replica from the Levi Strauss Museum of a pair that dates from about 1880. Boone's store would have sold jeans as well as denim, the fabric needed to make them.

While her parents are busy shopping, this girl has spotted a doll she would like to take home.

Noisy items like toy drums were especially popular—with kids if not their parents!

Fun and games

Children would have headed straight for the toy section in Boone's. Colored marbles, used to play a miniature version of bowling, were popular, as were toy weapons. Children used these to play at being soldiers in the US Civil War, which had ended 15 years before.

This man is waiting as a store clerk spins the wheels on the coffee grinder.

This doll carries a miniature ball and racket. She is dressed rather fancy for tennis.

The ceiling is decorated with patterned panels.

This store clerk has to climb a ladder to reach the upper shelves.

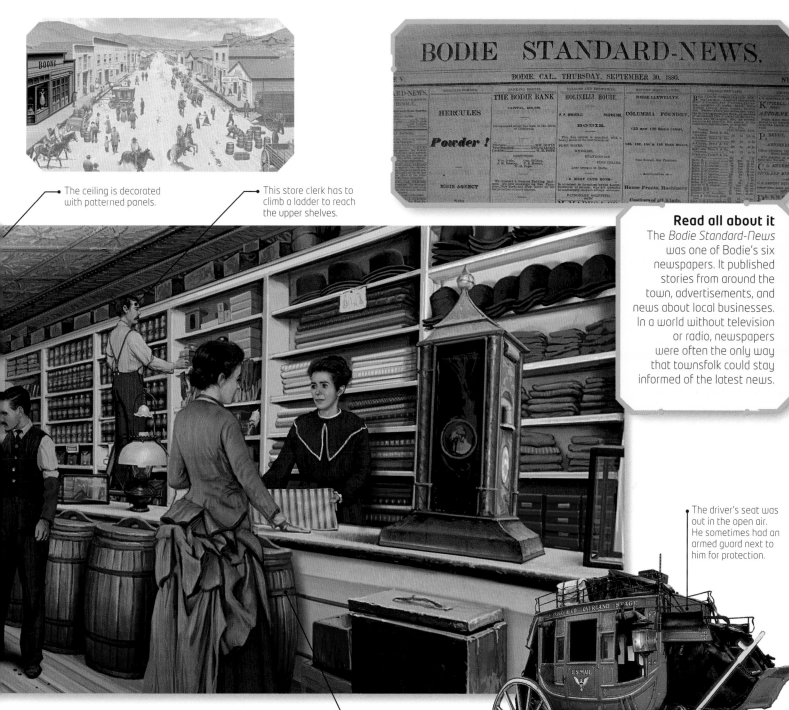

BODIE STANDARD-NEWS.

BODIE, CAL., THURSDAY, SEPTEMBER 30, 1880.

Read all about it

The *Bodie Standard-News* was one of Bodie's six newspapers. It published stories from around the town, advertisements, and news about local businesses. In a world without television or radio, newspapers were often the only way that townsfolk could stay informed of the latest news.

The driver's seat was out in the open air. He sometimes had an armed guard next to him for protection.

Goods like flour and sugar were stored in barrels.

Medicine
In many towns, the general store also functioned as a pharmacy. Boone's stocked medicines that promised to cure things like headaches, hay fever, indigestion, and even baldness.

Intercity transportation
Stagecoaches connected Bodie to the wider world. They picked up and dropped off mail and carried passengers to and from other cities. Coaches also carried bullion bars, a mixture of gold and silver from Bodie's mines, to mints where they would be processed into coins.

CHAMPION SALOON

After a hard shift at the mines and mills, Bodie's male residents head for one of the town's 60 or so saloon bars to socialize, discuss business, and relax. Inside, a saloon is a long, narrow, smoke-filled room where people could drink, gamble, enjoy a hot meal, and, sometimes, get into trouble. Today, a dispute at the Champion Saloon over the result of a card game is about to descend into a fully fledged bar brawl.

Musical entertainment
Many saloons kept a piano and some put on performances every night. Sometimes the pianist would be accompanied by a fiddle player or even a guitarist and a singer. This piano is still standing in the Sam Leon Bar, one of Bodie's remaining saloons.

1 This man can't believe that his quiet drink has been disturbed by someone trying to cheat at cards—again! .

Death in Bodie
Life on the frontier was full of risks. Lethal gunfights sometimes occurred in Bodie's saloons, and working in the mines was dangerous and often deadly work. Bodie's horse-drawn hearse had to make many trips carrying deceased people to funerals.

2 No one cheats this card player and gets away with it! He's so angry that he's drawn his pistol.

5 This spittoon is full of slimy lumps of chewed tobacco that guests have spat out.

Beating the dealer

Faro was the most popular card game in the west. Players competed against the dealer to match their cards to his. A fast and furious game, it was sometimes called "bucking the tiger," after the tiger design used on a popular brand of cards.

The cylinder could hold seven shots.

Weapon of choice

The revolvers most men carried in Bodie were short-barreled, like the British Bulldog pistol. This small gun could easily fit inside a coat pocket, which made it easy to hide and quick to draw if a fight broke out.

UNION HALL

Bodie's Miners Union Hall provided a place to meet and talk away from the noisy saloons. It is also where the miners worked to fight for—and win—the right to a fair wage of $4 a day.

3 Miners often come straight to the saloon after their shift. Many don't even change their dirty clothes.

4 The faro dealer has recently arrived in Bodie from the east. He is keeping a watchful eye over the players and his money.

6 The bartender is preparing to break up the fight. He's had to do this before so he's stashed a weapon under the bar.

STILL STOCKED UP

Boone's Store in the ghost town of Bodie still displays shelves full of goods, showing visitors what would have been on sale when the town was inhabited. Products on offer include groceries and alcohol, hay and grain for horses, and even tooth powder. Customers at Boone's could grind their newly purchased coffee beans at the wheeled machine by the front door.

TITANIC

Titanic was the biggest, fastest, most luxurious cruise ship ever built—and its designers said it was the safest, too. But on its first voyage, in April 1912, the ship hit an iceberg. Three hours later, it lay at the bottom of the ocean, and more than 1,500 people had lost their lives.

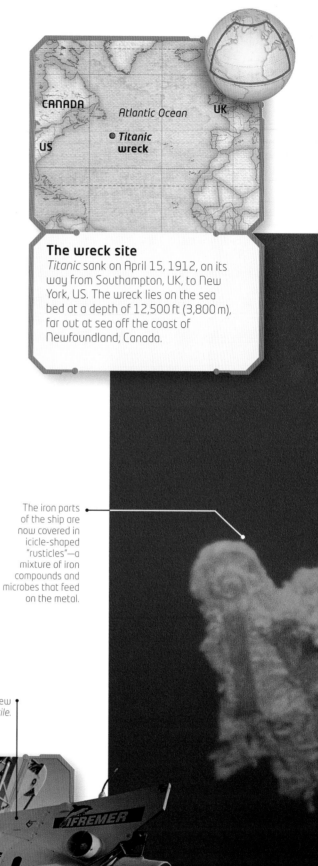

CANADA   Atlantic Ocean   UK

US   ● *Titanic* wreck

Building *Titanic*
Construction of *Titanic* began in March 1909 at the Harland & Wolff shipyard in Belfast, Northern Ireland. It was the second of the White Star Line's "superships"—the first to be completed was *Titanic's* sister ship, *Olympic* (seen here). The ships were so large that they had to be built in specially-made docks.

Three huge bronze propellers were fitted at the back of the ship to power it through the water.

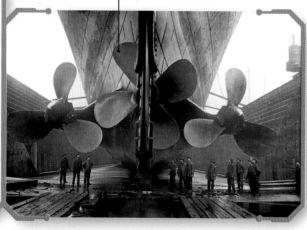

The wreck site
Titanic sank on April 15, 1912, on its way from Southampton, UK, to New York, US. The wreck lies on the sea bed at a depth of 12,500 ft (3,800 m), far out at sea off the coast of Newfoundland, Canada.

Preserved by the sea
Even after more than 100 years, much of the wreck is still intact. At this depth, it is so cold and the pressure so great that most of the plants, fish, or bacteria that would normally damage a wreck cannot survive.

The iron parts of the ship are now covered in icicle-shaped "rusticles"—a mixture of iron compounds and microbes that feed on the metal.

This porcelain bathtub is in the cabin of the captain, Edward Smith, who died in the tragedy.

There is space for three crew members aboard *Nautile*.

Finding the wreck
Titanic was only discovered in 1985, when a combined French/US expedition spotted one of the boilers. A short time later, they found the ship's bow (front), embedded in mud. Since then, submersibles like *Nautile* have brought hundreds of items up from the deep.

Floating giant
Titanic was truly vast. It had 10 decks and could carry up to 3,547 passengers and crew. It was 882½ ft (269 m) long—the length of 22 buses. When fully laden, it weighed 73,924 tons (67,063 metric tons).

There were 16 lifeboats, plus four collapsible dinghies—not enough for everyone on board.

The rear funnel didn't function— it was just for show, to make the ship look even more impressive.

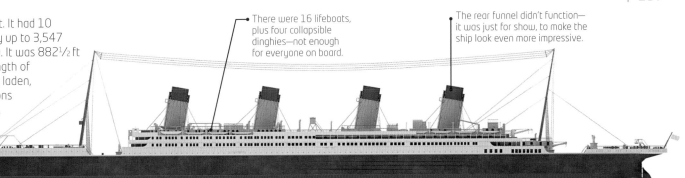

Undersea resting place
Titanic's bow lies on the sea bed, partly buried in thick mud. About 2,000 ft (600 m) away, facing the opposite direction, lies the ship's stern (back end). Weighed down by flooded compartments, the bow broke off from the rest of the ship and sank first. Contents spilled out over a debris field measuring about ¾ sq mile (2 sq km).

1 **Men go last**
A crewman tries to ensure that women and children board the lifeboats first.

2 **Save my child!**
A mother drops her baby into the lifeboat, knowing that she has little hope of escaping herself.

3 **Lowering the boats**
Crewmen winch the lifeboats down using ropes and pulleys on a small crane called a davit.

4 **Lifeboat 15**
One of the last lifeboats to launch, this boat eventually takes 70 people to safety.

5 **Lifeboat 13**
Men use oars to push their boat out of the way of Lifeboat 15, which is about to land on it.

6 **Deckchair overboard**
People throw deckchairs down so that the people in the water can use them as life rafts.

7 **Eerie glow**
The sea is glowing green with phosphorescence emitted by tiny marine organisms.

8 **Keeping the lights on**
The ship still has electrical power and lights thanks to the engineering crew's work.

9 **Swimming to safety**
Some passengers have jumped into the icy water and are trying to swim to the lifeboats.

10 **Sinking bow**
As the bow (front) slips below the water, those who can dash toward the ship's stern.

11 **Cry for help**
A distress rocket explodes like a firework, alerting any nearby ships that Titanic is in trouble.

SINKING FAST

Just before midnight on April 15, 1912, *Titanic* hit an iceberg that tore several holes in the ship's hull. Within minutes, sections of the ship were filling with water, dragging the front of the vessel down. As panicked passengers scrambled to get on lifeboats, the crew desperately tried to help passengers off the ship while they signaled for help. Within two hours, the doomed ship would lie at the bottom of the ocean.

Musical treasure
This violin, still in its case, was recovered soon after the sinking. It belonged to Wallace Henry Hartley, *Titanic's* bandleader, who did not survive. It is said that the band played cheerful tunes during the sinking to keep people's spirits up as they boarded the lifeboats.

CENTER OF THE SHIP

No expense was spared in making *Titanic* the most luxurious ocean liner ever seen. This may have given first-class passengers a false sense of security as the ship began to sink. Many of them felt safer on board and refused to wait for a lifeboat in the cold. But as the danger of the situation became clear, panic set in, and soon terrified passengers were gathering their possessions and racing to the lifeboat deck.

An exclusive experience
First-class diners could visit a range of restaurants, cafes, and bars. *À La Carte* was the most exclusive—passengers paid extra to enjoy French cuisine on elegant silverware and china, such as that shown here alongside a menu from *Titanic*.

1 This crewman is trying to direct panicking passengers to the lifeboat deck.

This silverware with White Star branding comes from *Titanic's* sister ships.

2 Some passengers, feeling safe on board, refuse to evacuate.

3 This man is desperately searching for his wife and daughter.

4 Passengers line up to reclaim their valuables from the Purser's Office where they had been stowed for safe keeping. Anything that is not claimed will sink to the bottom of the ocean.

Strolling on deck

Most of the top four decks were for the exclusive use of first-class guests. On "A" deck, passengers could enjoy the sea breeze along an open-air walkway. Part of it was covered, so strolls could be taken even when the weather was poor.

The glass dome allowed natural light to flood into the Grand Staircase.

The Grand Staircase

Titanic's Grand Staircase was the ship's centerpiece. It led all the way from the first-class promenade deck to the dining saloon on "D" deck. Lavishly decorated with solid oak panels, brass fittings, and crystal lighting, the staircase was topped by a huge glass and wrought-iron dome.

6 Waiters continue serving drinks to passengers who have decided to stay on board.

Privileged passengers

Those traveling in first class had a greater chance of surviving the disaster than others on board. Only 30% of those in first class lost their lives, compared to about 66% of the other classes and crew members.

Lady Duff-Gordon escaped on Lifeboat 1 with just 11 others. There was space for 40 people in the boat.

5 The elevator transporting first-class passengers from the promenade to the lower decks will soon be flooded.

RACE AGAINST TIME

Soon after *Titanic* hit the iceberg, it was clear that the ship was doomed. The challenge now was to keep the engines running and the lights on for long enough to get as many people as possible into lifeboats. A team of firemen and engineers battled to keep the ship going as, one by one, the boiler rooms filled with water.

Feeding the fires
The *Titanic* was powered by burning coal, which produced steam that drove the engines. The "black gang" of 289 firemen constantly shoveled coal into the 29 massive boilers to keep the engines running at full speed.

Each boiler room had a team of 14 men, feeding every boiler a ton of coal every two minutes.

First find
In 1985, as the *Titanic* discovery expedition, having failed to find the wreck, neared the end of its mission, a huge object appeared on the video feed from the ocean floor: one of the ship's boilers. After 73 years, *Titanic* had finally been found.

The boiler sat face-up, the circular furnace doors clearly visible.

1 *Titanic* had 29 of these colossal boilers, spread out over six boiler rooms.

2 The boilers have three coal-fired furnaces at each end.

The sinking ship

Titanic was thought to be virtually unsinkable because it was divided into watertight compartments. If two compartments flooded, the ship could stay afloat. But the iceberg made a series of gashes in the ship and water rushed into four compartments, soon spreading to a fifth. This was too much for *Titanic*.

Titanic's bulkheads were watertight walls between compartments.

The bulkheads only reached 10 ft (3 m) above the waterline, so as the ship tipped forward, water would soon slop over them and into more of the compartments.

Water from the first four compartments, poured into the fifth before the doors could be closed.

"**Water came pouring in** two feet above the [floor]; the ship's **side was torn** from the third [boiler room] to the forward end."

—Frederick William Barrett, Lead stoker

Frederick Barrett
Lead fireman Frederick Barrett was on duty in boiler room six when the collision happened. He escaped on Lifeboat 13, but it drifted under Lifeboat 15, which was being lowered into the sea. Barrett pushed his boat clear, saving many lives with his actions.

3 The water seeping up through the floor poses a deadly risk: if the boilers flood, so much steam will be produced that they might explode.

4 The crewmen have to work quickly to reduce the fires and vent the steam the boilers produce to reduce the chance of an explosion.

5 The engineer in charge of the team is sending updates to the captain up on the bridge.

IN THE DEEP

The submersible *Mir* approaches the bow of the *Titanic*, about 12,500 ft (3,800 m) below sea level.. Three people can fit inside *Mir*, although it is so cramped that two of them have to lie down. *Mir* connects to smaller robotic submersibles that can venture inside *Titanic's* nooks and crannies.

THE FIRST WORLD WAR

At the outbreak of World War I (1914–1918) in Europe, both sides built trenches to defend their positions. Neither the Allies (led by Britain and France) nor the Central Powers (led by Germany) could strike a decisive blow. The Battle of Messines in 1917 was a major attack by the Allies, which used underground mines planted beneath German trenches. Today, archaeologists are still finding clothing, weapons, and other evidence of the fights that raged until the Allies broke through.

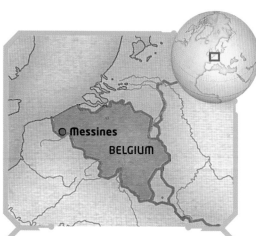

Battle plans
Messines Ridge was a 264-ft- (80-m-) high hill in German-occupied Belgium, close to the border with France. The Allies planned to break through the German lines and capture the Belgian coastline.

Lasting memory
Some craters from the Messines blasts still exist. The biggest, at Spanbroekmolen, was made when 90,000 lb (40,823 kg) of explosives went off. It is now called the "Pool of Peace."

Dummy tree
Allied soldiers had several ways of gathering information on the enemy including this dummy tree used by Australian troops. It was made of metal and canvas, and a soldier equipped with binoculars hid inside to spy on German soldiers.

The "tree" was made to look like it had been shot at and bombed.

Space was very tight and it was extremely uncomfortable inside the dummy tree.

Mobile weapons
The Allies used powerful cannons called howitzers to fire thousands of shells during the attack. Also called field guns, there were 108 of these smaller, wheeled howitzers at Messines and 214 larger howitzers.

Wheels allowed soldiers to move the cannon to where it was needed most on the battlefield.

Trench design
Trenches were cut in zig-zag patterns rather than straight lines. This meant that if any enemy attackers got inside they could not shoot along the entire length of the trench.

Defensive lines
The Allied attack at Messines took place along a 9¾-mile (16-km) front, but the heaviest fighting was at the long, low hill known as Messines Ridge. Today, the area is mostly farmland—as it was before the war—but in some places landowners have allowed archaeologists to dig up the site. This replica trench has been built at a nearby site.

Support structure
Trench walls were made of earth and sometimes collapsed. They were strengthened with wooden planks, wicker branches, or corrugated iron.

Duckboards
Trench floors were lined with wooden slats called duckboards that helped keep soldiers' feet dry. Troops who stood in mud and water too long suffered from a rotting condition called trench foot.

Extra firepower
The German trench systems included concrete "pillboxes" with machine guns on top to fire on enemy attacks. They were usually square, with a slit at the front for defenders to fire from.

MESSINES TRENCH

At exactly 3:10 am on June 7, 1917, 19 huge mines planted in tunnels dug by Allied sappers (engineers) explode under the feet of German soldiers defending Messines Ridge, while shells rain down. At the same moment, Allied tanks and troops begin an assault on the German trenches in an attempt to push them back.

1 Allied army
Troops from Britain, Ireland, Australia, and New Zealand storm the German lines.

2 The battlefield
This muddy mess of craters and burned trees between trenches is known as No-Man's-Land.

3 Powerful weapons
Heavy guns fire 60-lb (27-kg) shells at the German trenches, aiming to destroy their artillery.

4 Bulletproof
Bullets bounce off this British Mark IV tank as it crawls toward the enemy trench.

5 Fix bayonets!
Allied soldiers leap down into the trench, preparing for close combat with the enemy.

6 Lighting up
This flare brightens the night sky. Its light helps defenders spot approaching troops.

7 German engineering
Trench defenses include sandbags, strong walls, shelters, and raised steps to shoot from.

8 Taken by surprise
These soldiers were relaxing when the attack began. They need to get into position fast!

9 Communications
Soldiers used "field telephones" connected by wire to contact HQ. Often wires were cut.

10 Dogfighting
High overhead, Allied S.E.5as and Sopwith Triplanes battle German Albatros D.IIIs.

11 Boom!
These explosions are caused by mines planted in tunnels deep below the trenches.

LIFE ON THE FRONT

Daily life in the trenches is either very boring or very dangerous. For many German soldiers, cave-like dugouts lining the trench walls are safe spaces to relax between battles. Meanwhile, above ground, troops use deadly machine guns hidden inside concrete "pillboxes" to fight off enemy attacks.

The dugout
Areas carved from the trench wall where soldiers sheltered from bombs or rested at quiet times were called dugouts. German dugouts were often deeper and better built than Allied ones.

Both Allied and German troops use millions of sandbags to protect themselves from gunfire and exploding shells. Each bag of sand weighs about 40 lb (18 kg).

Card games
Playing cards was a popular way to keep boredom at bay. Toy makers produced cards for the troops decorated with military images, as on this Swiss set.

Soldiers have to rest, make coffee, or take a nap whenever they can, as they never know when the enemy will strike next.

Home comforts
Some German troops built "luxury" dugouts, which were almost homelike, with signs over their doorways that said things like "Home Sweet Home." A few had two or even three underground levels.

Men use a tin cooking dish to boil water or cook food over small heaters.

Writing and receiving letters reminds soldiers of their loved ones at home.

Rats
There were more rats than soldiers in the trenches. They stole food and spread disease. Both sides used dogs, especially terriers, to hunt the rodent invaders.

Rapid fire

The *Maschinengewehr 08*, or MG08, was the German Army's main machine gun. It fired 400 rounds a minute to a distance of 1¼ miles (2 km). The ammunition was fed into the gun on belts, each of which held 250 bullets.

The MG08 was an automatic gun, meaning it kept firing until the trigger was released.

A pin was put through these holes to angle the gun up or down.

Head gear

The *Stahlhelm* "coal scuttle" helmet was used by German troops in World Wars I and II. The side holes were for ventilation. In winter, soldiers stuffed the holes with mud or cloth to keep out cold air.

"**Trench fighting** is the **bloodiest, wildest, most brutal** of all .... There's no mercy there, **no going back** ..."

—Ernst Jünger, German officer (1895-1998)

Pillboxes

Enemy troops were terrified of attacking pillboxes—the nonstop gunfire from these raised positions was deadly. But pillboxes were also vulnerable to bombs and bullets.

Troops use binoculars to watch their enemies approach.

Soldiers carry spare ammunition in belts.

German long boots are known as marching boots.

Handgun

This long-barreled pistol called a Luger was often carried by German artillery officers instead of a rifle.

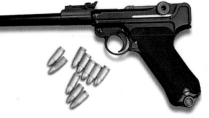

Wooden and metal boxes protect ammunition from damage and made sure it stayed dry.

This man's job is to load the machine gun's ammunition quickly and make sure the weapon does not jam.

MIGHTY MACHINES

German troops must have been terrified at the sight of a Mark IV tank rumbling toward them, especially as their rifle bullets often pinged off its armor as it slowly but unstoppably approached, its powerful guns blasting. But the Mark IV is not invincible. Thick mud and steep slopes cause it as much trouble as German missiles, and being inside one is a hot, sweaty, uncomfortable, and dangerous experience.

Six-pounder gun
There were two types of Mark IV tank. One had a large gun on each side that fired six-pound shells. The other had two machine guns on each side instead, making it useful in close combat against infantry troops.

The roof had one entrance hatch for eight crew members: a driver, commander, two side gunners, two loaders, and two brake operators.

The tank's 105 hp (horse power) Daimler engine could reach a top speed of just 3.69 mph (5.95 km/h).

The bulge on the tank's side was called a sponson. It allowed the gun to rotate and find its target more easily.

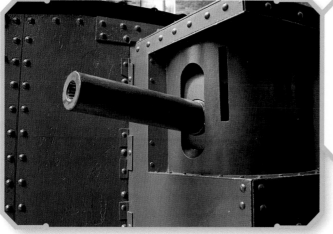

"It was a **complete and utter surprise** to the Germans that we **ever devised** such a thing as a **tank**."

—Monty Cleeve, British artillery officer (1894-1993)

Heavy ammunition
Mark IV tanks carried around 300 shells for their six-pounder guns. They could be fired a distance of more than 4¼ miles (7 km) and each one was 19 in (48 cm) long and 3 in (7.6 cm) in diameter.

The Mark IV's armor was ½ in (12 mm) thick. This made it bulletproof, but heavy artillery fire could stop it in its tracks.

Pedal power
The tank's commander and driver sat at the front of the tank. The commander used pedals to control the tank's speed, and the driver used levers to turn the tank by stopping one of the two sets of tracks.

LITTLE WILLIE

The first working tank model was designed by the British Royal Navy rather than the Army and was originally known as a "Landship" or a "Land Caterpillar." It was built in 1915 and nicknamed "Little Willie." After some design changes, its size and shape changed to that of the Mark IV, so Little Willie is the only example of its kind ever built.

The Mark IV's commander was also in charge of the forward weapon, which was either a Lewis or Hotchkiss machine gun.

After the debut of the Mark IV at Messines, another 1,200 were built. It saw the most action of any tank in the war.

Stuck in the mud
If a tank got trapped in mud, its crew had to hitch a long, rectangular wooden and metal pole called an unditching beam to the front of its tracks. This made a solid surface that the tank was able to drive over and free itself.

At 26 ft 3 in (8 m), Mark IVs were as long as a bus. They were 13 ft 6 in (4.11 m) wide and 7 ft 11 in (2.43 m) tall.

INTERNATIONAL ARMIES
These soldiers in the French army traveled from Africa to Europe to fight in World War I. At the outbreak of war, France and Britain called on people living in their overseas colonies for aid. Approximately 2.5 million troops from Africa and 1.5 million from India fought in the conflict.

GLOSSARY

Allies
People or countries working together. In World War I and World War II, the Allies were the countries fighting Germany and other forces.

Ammunition
Objects fired or propelled from a weapon, such as bullets.

Amulet
A small object believed to ward off evil spirits, illness, or danger.

Anglo-Saxon
The people who lived in England from the 5th century and ruled large parts of it until the Norman conquest in 1066.

Ancestor
A person who lived in the past, and who is a distant relative of people who are alive today.

Aqueduct
A special channel (either raised up or buried underground) that carries water.

Archaeologist
A person who excavates sites to reveal their history by studying the objects and human remains found there.

Artillery
Large guns used in warfare.

Artifact
An object made by someone, such as a beautiful vase or a useful pot or tool.

Artisan
A skilled craftsperson producing things by hand.

Autopsy
Examination of a dead body performed by a trained pathologist to find out how the person might have died.

Bacteria
Tiny microscopic life forms that live all around us; some can cause disease and infections.

BCE
A term meaning "Before the Common Era," placed after a date to indicate it happened before year 0, which is the start of the "Common Era," or CE.

Bullion
A bar of precious metal, such as silver or gold.

Calligraphy
Handwriting as a highly valued art form, especially in Arabic, Chinese, and Japanese script.

Caravan
A train of animals, usually camels, used to transport goods across long distances. Camel caravans were often used on the Silk Roads.

Cast
A copy of an original artifact, made by pouring plaster into a mold. In archaeology, plaster is poured into holes formed in the earth when bodies and artifacts buried there have decayed.

CE
Abbreviation for "Common Era," used in dates (see BCE).

Citizen
A person who belongs to a city or a bigger community, such a state or country, and has certain rights.

City-state
A city, and its surrounding territory, that has its own independent government.

Civil war
A war fought between inhabitants of the same country.

Colony
An area under the political and economic control of another state, usually in a foreign country.

Culture
The customs, beliefs, and behavior shared by a society.

Deity
A god or a goddess.

Diplomat
A person appointed by a country or other political body to carry out negotiations and maintain relationships with other countries.

Dogfight
A close battle between two fighter planes, especially in World War I and II.

Dynasty
A family ruling a country for successive generations.

Emperor/Empress
The absolute ruler of an empire.

Empire
A group of lands or peoples under the rule of a single government or person.

Excavate
In archaeology, to dig up an area in an organized way in order to find remains of buildings, people, and artifacts.

Excavation
An area being dug up for archaeological purposes.

Extinct
Describes a species that has no living members.

Fortress
See Fortification

Fortification
A strong building or set of buildings designed to withstand attacks and protect the people inside.

Forensic
Describes work carried out by scientists to help solve crimes.

Fresco
Art painted directly on a wet plaster wall.

Frieze
A decorative carving running along the upper part of the wall of a building.

Galleon
A type of three-masted ship used in the 15th–17th centuries.

Glacier
A large, slow-moving mass of ice on land, often through a mountain valley.

Government
A group of people governing a country, often (but not always) elected to do so.

Gothic
A style of architecture popular in medieval Europe from the 12th century, featuring soaring spires and pointy arches. Also refers to the religious art of that period.

HQ (Headquarters)
In World War I, the place where military commanders stayed, planned, and oversaw the operations on the battlefield.

Immigrant
A person leaving one nation to move to another country and settle there.

Import
The purchase of goods and services from other countries.

Infantry
A part of an army made up of soldiers fighting on foot.

Kingdom
A state or area ruled over by a king or queen.

Loincloth
A piece of fabric or animal skin tied around the hips.

Mangrove
A tree that grows in shallow water and on low shores by the sea or in river estuaries in tropical regions, with roots growing above ground.

Manuscript
A document written by hand; the common form of book before printing was invented.

Medieval
Describes anything dating from or taking place during the 6th to the 15th centuries, especially in Europe.

Merchant
A person who buys or sells goods.

Mosaic
A decoration made from small pieces of glass, stone, or tile stuck into position to make a picture or pattern.

Mughals
The Muslim people who ruled large parts of India from 1526 to the mid-19th century.

Mummification
The process of preserving a dead body to prevent it from decaying. Mummification can also occur naturally when bodies are exposed to certain conditions.

Neolithic
The later Stone Age, during which improved stone weapons were made and the first farming began.

Noble
A member of the nobility or aristocracy, with more rights and privileges than people who were peasants or merchants.

Palaestra
A school for wrestling in ancient Greece and Rome.

Pavilion
A small building, often made to be decorative rather than just practical, and with a roof resting on pillars instead of walls.

Peasant
A worker on the land, usually an agricultural laborer.

Petroglyph
A carving or painting made on a rock.

Pharaoh
A title given to a king in ancient Egypt. People believed that pharaohs had sacred powers and were descended from the sun god, Ra.

Pictogram
See Petroglyph

Pilgrim
A religious person who makes a journey to a holy place.

Pilgrimage
A religious journey to a holy place.

Plantation
A farm or estate on which cotton, tobacco, coffee, rice, hops, or other crops are grown.

Province
A part of a country or empire which often has the right to rule itself to some degree.

Quarry
A place where rocks and minerals are dug or hacked out from the ground.

Ranch
A large farm where horses, sheep, or cattle are bred, especially in the Americas.

Sacred
Considered holy and with religious significance, possibly related to a god or goddess.

Sanctuary
A holy or sacred place, such as a temple or church. Also a place where people could seek shelter and protection.

Scripture
Sacred writings of any religion, such as the Christian Bible.

Scythian
A person from Scythia, a historic region on the grasslands north of ancient Persia.

Sentry
A soldier who is on guard or watch duty.

Settlers
People from a region or country who move into another region or country that is new to them, often on land already settled by an indigenous population.

Settlement
A place where people have settled down and built homes.

Shrine
A building or place considered sacred and usually dedicated to a god, spirit, or holy object.

Siege
The surrounding and blockading (blocking entrances and exits) of a castle, town, or other fortified structure in order to capture it.

Silk Roads
Several trade routes from China to West Asia and Europe, named after the most valuable product traded, silk.

Slavery
The system of owning people as property. Enslaved people have no rights and work with no pay.

Smelting
A process used to extract metals from rocks, known as ore, containing them.

Society
A group of people who live together or who are involved together in a community.

State
A country, or region within a country, which has its own government

Sultan
Title of a ruler of some Muslim countries or regions.

Temple
A building for religious worship or ceremonies.

Territory
A geographic area that has come under the control of a government.

INDEX

ACKNOWLEDGMENTS

DK would like to thank:
Elizabeth Wise for the index; Danielle Cluer Gee for proofreading; Simon Mumford for the maps; Chrissy Barnard for design help.

The publisher would also like to thank the following for their kind permission to reproduce their photographs:

(Key: a-above; b-below/bottom; c-centre; cl-centre left; fcl-far centre left; cr-centre right; cra-centre right above; clb-centre left below; crb-centre right below; tc-top centre; br-below/bottom right; f-far; l-left; r-right; t-top; tl-top left; tr-top right;)

6 Alamy Stock Photo: mikeobiz (bl); Panther Media GmbH (cl). Getty Images: Xavier Desmier (t); Anna Gorin (br). 7 Alamy Stock Photo: Ulrich Doering (bl); Hemis (tl); Ian Littlewood (tr). Dreamstime.com: Anton Aleksenko (c). Getty Images: R.M. Nunes (br). 8 Alamy Stock Photo: CTK (tc); James King-Holmes (cr). Getty Images: DEA / A. Dagli Orti (bl); Mittnik et al.: (cl). 9 Alamy Stock Photo: Album (br). Shutterstock.com: zedspider. 11 Alamy Stock Photo: blickwinkel (b); Ian Dagnall (tl); The Natural History Museum (c). Dorling Kindersley. Getty Images: DEA / A. Dagli Orti (cb). 12-13 Alamy Stock Photo: agefotostock. 14 Alamy Stock Photo: Sanja Radosavljevic (cl/sloe berries). Science Photo Library: PAUL D Stewart (cr). South Tyrol Museum Of Archaeology - www.iceman.it: Eurac / Samadelli / Staschitz (b). 14-15 Getty Images: Paul Hanny. 15 Alamy Stock Photo: mauritius images GmbH (br). 17 Bridgeman Images: © Wolfgang Neeb (t); © Wolfgang Neeb (cl). South Tyrol Museum Of Archaeology - www.iceman.it: Eurac / Samadelli / Staschitz (cr); Harald Wisthaler (b). 18 Alamy Stock Photo: (br); Heritage Image Partnership Ltd (c). Bridgeman Images: Sandro Vannini (cl). 18-19 Dreamstime.com: Anton Aleksenko (t). 19 Alamy Stock Photo: History & Art Collection (br); robertharding (bc). 22 Getty Images: DEA / A. Jemolo (bl). 23 Alamy Stock Photo: robertharding (cr). Bridgeman Images: Harvard University-Boston Museum of Fine Arts Expedition (br). Dorling Kindersley: Peter Harper / © The Trustees of the British Museum. All rights reserved. (tr). 24 Alamy Stock Photo: Jose Lucas (cl). Bridgeman Images: NPL - DeA Picture Library (bl). Getty Images: Christophel Fine Art (bc). 25 akg-images: Heritage Images / Ashmolean Museum, University of Oxford (br). © The Trustees of the British Museum. All rights reserved.: (tr). Getty Images: swisshippo (tc). 26 Bridgeman Images: Harvard University-Boston Museum of Fine Arts Expedition (bc); Sandro Vannini (bl). 27 akg-images: De Agostini Picture Lib. / G. Dagli Orti (br). Alamy Stock Photo: agefotostock (tc). Bridgeman Images: Werner Forman Archive (tr). 28-29

Bridgeman Images: NPL - DeA Picture Library / S. Vannini. 30 akg-images: Bible Land Pictures (b). Alamy Stock Photo: Tuul and Bruno Morandi (cl); The Print Collector (cr). 30-31 Alamy Stock Photo: INTERFOTO (tr). 31 Alamy Stock Photo: The Print Collector (br). Getty Images: Photo Josse / Leemage (bl). 32 Alamy Stock Photo: Album (tr); Ivan Vdovin (tl); INTERFOTO (c); Zip Lexing (b). 34-35 Alamy Stock Photo: Tibor Bognar. 36 akg-images: (l). Bridgeman Images: Look and Learn (br). 36-37 Getty Images: Posnov (tr). 37 Alamy Stock Photo: INTERFOTO (br). Getty Images: Heritage Images (bc). 40 Alamy Stock Photo: Ancient Art and Architecture (cl). © The Trustees of the British Museum. All rights reserved.. Getty Images: DEA / A. Dagli Orti (bl). 41 akg-images: jh-Lightbox_Ltd. / John Hios (br); Erich Lessing (cr). Alamy Stock Photo: PRISMA ARCHIVO (tr). 42 akg-images: MMA / Gift of George F. Baker / SCIENCE SOURCE (bl). 43 akg-images: jh-Lightbox_Ltd. / John Hios (bl); jh-Lightbox_Ltd. / John Hios (br). Alamy Stock Photo: Ivy Close Images (tr). 44 Alamy Stock Photo: agefotostock (cl); Pump Park Vintage Photography (bl); Athikhun Boonrin (cr); RichardBakerItaly (bc). Dorling Kindersley: James Stevenson / Museo Archeologico Nazionale di Napoli (c). 45 Alamy Stock Photo: Granger Historical Picture Archive (br). 48 Alamy Stock Photo: Azoor Travel Photo (bl). Dorling Kindersley: James Stevenson / Museo Archeologico Nazionale di Napoli (tr). 49 Alamy Stock Photo: Eye Ubiquitous (tr); robertharding (bl); Science History Images (br). 52 Dorling Kindersley: Dreamstime.com: Alvaro German Vilela (clb); James Stevenson / Museo Archeologico Nazionale di Napoli (tl); James Stevenson / Museo Archeologico Nazionale di Napoli (cr). Getty Images: DEA / L. PEDICINI (b). 53 Alamy Stock Photo: Chronicle (tr); ONOKY - Photononstop (cr). 54 Alamy Stock Photo: Heritage Image Partnership Ltd (bl). DigVentures: (cl); Durham University (br). 54-55 DigVentures. 55 Bridgeman Images: (br). DigVentures: Durham University (cr). 58 Alamy Stock Photo: The Picture Art Collection (br). Bridgeman Images: British Library Board. All Rights Reserved (tl). Shutterstock.com: Alfredo Dagli Orti (cl). 59 akg-images: Heritage Images / Heritage Art (tc). Alamy Stock Photo: Daegrad Photography (tl); INTERFOTO (tr). DigVentures: Durham University (b). 60 Alamy Stock Photo: Science History Images (c). Dorling Kindersley: Peter Anderson / Universitets Oldsaksamling, Oslo (cra); Dave King / Museum of London (cla). 61 Alamy Stock Photo: Science History Images (tr). 62-63 akg-images: Pictures From History. 64-65 Alamy Stock Photo: robertharding. 64 akg-images. Alamy Stock Photo: Nila Newsom (cr). 65 Alamy Stock Photo: Jake Lyell (br). 66 Alamy Stock Photo: dave stamboulis (b); Igor Zhorov (tr). Getty Images: Selina Yau (tl). 68 Alamy Stock Photo: Ulrich Doering (cl). Classical

Numismatic Group, LLC.: (bl). Marilee Wood: (cr). S. Wynne-Jones/Songo Mnara Urban Landscape Project: (br). 69 Alamy Stock Photo: Ulrich Doering; Jason Gallier (cr). 71 Alamy Stock Photo: Heritage Image Partnership Ltd (c); Eric Lafforgue (tr); NSP-RF (bl). © The Trustees of the British Museum. All rights reserved.. 72 Alamy Stock Photo: Nic Hamilton Photographic (crb). Bridgeman Images. 73 Alamy Stock Photo: Historic Collection (r/inset); Hemis. 80-81 Shutterstock.com: Kharbine-Tapabor. 82 Alamy Stock Photo: Metta image (tl). Bridgeman Images. Crow Canyon Archaeological Center: Wendy Mimiaga (cl). 83 Alamy Stock Photo: Zachary Frank (r/inset); mikeobiz. 84 Alamy Stock Photo: Cultural Archive (cl); Chuck Place (bl); Jean Williamson (bc). Getty Images: Doug Meek (tl). 86 Dorling Kindersley: iStock: joakimbkk (crb). Getty Images: DEA / A. Dagli Orti (cl). Shutterstock.com: DeltaOFF (bl). 86-87 Getty Images: R.M. Nunes (t). Shutterstock.com: Dmitry Rukhlenko (bc). 87 Alamy Stock Photo: agefotostock (br). 88 Alamy Stock Photo: Charles O. Cecil (tl); Veeravong Komalamena (tr). Bridgeman Images: Pictures from History / David Henley (bl). Shutterstock.com: Dale Warren (cl). 90 Alamy Stock Photo: Granger Historical Picture Archive (cr); Lordprice Collection (cl, c); IanDagnall Computing (bl). 90-91 Getty Images: Anna Gorin. 91 Getty Images: Austin Hou (br). 94 © The Metropolitan Museum of Art: (c). 95 Alamy Stock Photo: Zoonar GmbH (tl). Dorling Kindersley: Gary Ombler / University of Pennsylvania Museum of Archaeology and Anthropology (bl). 96 Alamy Stock Photo: Unlisted Images, Inc. (br). Getty Images: Markus Daniel (cr). 97 Bridgeman Images: Giancarlo Costa (br). Getty Images: Romina Moscovich / EyeEm (bl). 98-99 Getty Images: Istvan Kadar Photography. 100-101 Getty Images: DEA / W. BUSS (bl); DEA / W. BUSS (b/inset). 100 Alamy Stock Photo: CPA Media Pte Ltd (cl). 101 Alamy Stock Photo: V&A Images (bc). Bridgeman Images. 103 Alamy Stock Photo: Archive PL (bc); Historic Images (cr). Dreamstime.com: Jasonjung (tr). © The Metropolitan Museum of Art. 104 akg-images. Alamy Stock Photo: History & Art Collection (bl); Michael Snell (cl). 104-105 Alamy Stock Photo: Panther Media GmbH (t). 105 akg-images. Alamy Stock Photo: BIOSPHOTO (bl). 107 Alamy Stock Photo: ap-photo (br); BIOSPHOTO (tr); Rosanne Tackaberry (c). 108-109 naturepl.com: Oriol Alamany. 110 Alamy Stock Photo: Album (cr); coward_lion (cl); The History Collection (bl); Art2010 (br). 110-111 Shutterstock.com: Kenan Yarici (t). 111 Alamy Stock Photo. 113 Alamy Stock Photo: Artokoloro (c); Oleksiy Maksymenko Photography (tr); B. David Cathell (bl); Heritage Image Partnership Ltd (br). 114 Alamy Stock Photo: Zvonimir Atletić (bl); Alexey Borodin (cla); Imaginechina Limited (cl); PlanetNextDoor (br). 114-115 Alamy Stock Photo: Ian Littlewood (t). 115 Alamy Stock Photo:

Brent Hofacker (br); ZUMA Press, Inc. (bl). 118 Alamy Stock Photo: Betty Johnson (bl); LEJEANVRE Philippe (tl). 119 Alamy Stock Photo: CPA Media Pte Ltd (cr); PhotoStock-Israel (br). 120 Alamy Stock Photo: Don Bartell (cl); Jon Bower China (bl). 121 Alamy Stock Photo: Artokoloro (tc); Artokoloro (cr); BTEU / RKMLGE (br). 122 SavyBoat Models. 123 Getty Images: (br); Richard T. Nowitz (bl). Library of Congress, Washington, D.C.: (2007629014) (tc). Shutterstock.com: Steven Senne / AP (cr). Marie Zahn: (tr). 125 Getty Images: (cr, bl); Kathryn Scott Osler (br). Marie Zahn. 126 Alamy Stock Photo: Joanna Kalafatis (bl); Shelly Rivoli (cl); Dan Leeth (cr). Getty Images: Education Images (br). 126-127 Getty Images: Anna Henly (t). 127 Alamy Stock Photo: CPA Media Pte Ltd (br). 130 Alamy Stock Photo: dpa picture alliance (cl); David Wall (tc); INTERFOTO (bc, br). 131 Alamy Stock Photo: Noella Ballenger (bc). Dorling Kindersley: Neil Lukas (br). Michael H. Piatt. 132 Alamy Stock Photo: Unlisted Images, Inc. (cl). Dustin LeBrun: (bl). 133 Alamy Stock Photo: History & Art Collection (tr). Library of Congress, Washington, D.C.: (HABS CAL,26-BODI,2) (br). Michael H. Piatt: (cr). 134-135 Lori Hibbett. 136 Alamy Stock Photo: World History Archive (ca). Getty Images: Xavier Desmier (b). NOAA: Courtesy of Lori_Johnston RMS Titanic Expedition 2003 (cb). 136-137 Getty Images: Xavier Desmier (b). 137 Alamy Stock Photo: Panther Media GmbH (t). 144-145 Alamy Stock Photo: Everett Collection Inc. 146 Alamy Stock Photo: David Crossland (cl). Dorling Kindersley: Gary Ombler / Royal Artillery Museum, Royal Artillery Historical Trust (bl). Imperial War Museum: (Q_031465) (cr). 146-147 Alamy Stock Photo: Arterra Picture Library. 147 Alamy Stock Photo: Guido Vermeulen-Perdaen (br). 150 Alamy Stock Photo: dpa picture alliance (br); INTERFOTO (cr). 151 Alamy Stock Photo: INTERFOTO (tc); Panther Media GmbH (tr); Militarist (br). 152 Alamy Stock Photo: Paul Cox (tl). Imperial War Museum: (MUN_003239) (bl). 153 Alamy Stock Photo: Insook Gardiner (tr). Dorling Kindersley: Gary Ombler / Imperial War Museum (tc). Imperial War Museum: (Q_011655) (br). 154-155 Getty Images: adoc-photos.

All other images © Dorling Kindersley